LIFE in Camelot

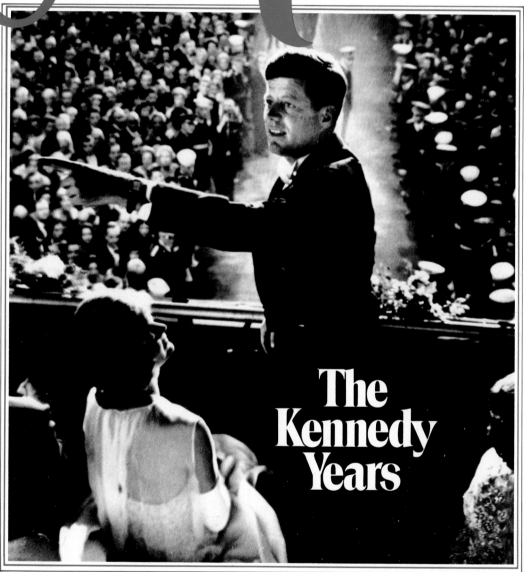

The Kennedy Years

Edited by Philip B. Kunhardt Jr.

LITTLE, BROWN AND COMPANY
BOSTON   TORONTO

CONTENTS

Edited by **Philip B. Kunhardt Jr.**

Written by **Philip B. Kunhardt Jr. and Frank K. Kappler**

Design and Production: **Gene Light**

Editorial Coordinator: **Gedeon de Margitay**

Research: **Elsie B. Washington**

Picture Research: **Gretchen Wessels**

*For their help in the creation of this book
we would also like to acknowledge:*

Beth B. Zarcone,
Chief, Time-Life Picture Collection

Peter Christopoulos,
Chief, Time-Life Photo Lab

*Also thanks to Richard B. Stolley, former
managing editor of LIFE and Roger
Herrmann, former general manager of LIFE,
both of whom helped shape this book.*

FIRST EDITION
Library of Congress Cataloging-in-Publication Data
   Life in Camelot: the Kennedy years / edited by Philip B. Kunhardt, Jr. — 1st ed.
      p.   cm.   ISBN 0-316-21089-7

   1. Kennedy, John F. (John Fitzgerald), 1917-1963 — Pictorial works.
   2. Presidents — United States — Pictorial works.   I. Kunhardt, Philip B.
   E842.L53 1988
   973.922'092'4 — dc 19
   [B]   88-3640   CIP
Published simultaneously in Canada by Little, Brown & Company (Canada) Limited
Acknowledgments to photographers and illustrators, including permission to reprint previously copyrighted material, appear on pages 318-319.
PRINTED IN THE UNITED STATES OF AMERICA

For more than 50 years now, each time a LIFE photographic assignment has been made, the film has been catalogued and the prints stored in the LIFE (now Time-Life) Picture Collection.

Between 1948 and 1963 the life and times of John F. Kennedy were tracked by 433 such assignments. These are a few of the typical Kennedy file cards that led to most of the pictures in this book.

THE MAKING OF A LEGEND

John
what powerful allie
his working style

and his private family life. Before
Kennedy, photographers covering
the White House were limited to official functions—greeting visiting
dignitaries, banquets, speeches,
document signings, presidential
comings and goings. The private
living room, the nursery, the vacation retreat, parties, intimate con-
ferences and the process of decision making were all off limits.

Throughout Kennedy's political
career LIFE was the world's biggest
and most prestigious picture magazine, so it was not surprising that
he put a special premium upon appearing in its pages. The magazine,
in turn, took advantage whenever
it could of Kennedy's friendly cooperation and the special access he
and his family afforded its photographers. The result was an extraordi-

A staff photographer working out of the
magazine's Washington bureau, Ed Clark
had taken one of the most famous pictures
of Senator Kennedy—little daughter
Caroline peeking out at him from her
bassinet. While photographing Kennedy a
few years later in the Oval Office, Ed spotted
his Caroline picture
in a frame high up on
a bookshelf. Would
the President
pose with the picture?
Up jumped Kennedy
on a chair,
grabbed the
photograph, leapt
down and obligingly
posed. This kind of
friendly, easygoing
cooperation between
Kennedy and LIFE's
photographers led to
many pictures that
would never
have been made
under former, more
formal White
House press etiquette.
This picture of Clark's
is published here
and on the
back jacket for the
first time.

by Philip B. Kunhardt Jr.

ennedy was the first President to realize
hotographs could be, especially ones showing

nary picture history of what turned out to be the paramount saga of our times.

LIFE in Camelot marks the first time this unparalleled LIFE resource has been drawn upon to tell the story of John F. Kennedy's life. All the pictures in this book were published by LIFE or were taken for the magazine. Some of the photographs are only too familiar historic landmarks, indelibly engraved upon the nation's soul. Others, published on LIFE's pages over a period of half a century, have long since been forgotten. Still others, more than a hundred in number, have never been published before, many never even printed up from their negatives, which have been carefully stored in the magazine's archives.

No other publication covered the J.F.K. years as diligently as did LIFE. The magazine spotted him early, recorded his meteoric rise, captured his family life with imagination and flair, followed his every step during his run for the presidency and virtually never left his side in all his public moments when he was in office. And it was there for many private ones. A LIFE photographer was either at the White House or on 24-hour alert during the home days of Kennedy's presidency; when he traveled a LIFE team was at his heels. Sometimes these efforts provided nothing worth publishing. At other times the pictures were noteworthy but the magazine didn't have the space to use them. "Protective coverage" we called it—just in case.

In the files of LIFE's Picture Collection there are listed 433 individual photographic assignments on John Kennedy alone, and there were hundreds more on other members of his family—his father, his mother, his wife, his brothers and

sisters, his children and more recently the slew of Kennedy offspring now confusing us all by their very number.

The family began to attract LIFE's attention back in 1937 when the magazine was only a year old. In a posed family portrait, all 11 Kennedys smiled across two pages with the headline NINE CHILDREN AND NINE MILLION DOLLARS.

Big, rich, good-looking families always beguiled LIFE. The variety of their activities and their sumptuous settings and life-styles were ideal for pictures. In addition, the Kennedy children had a shrewd, outspoken father who wielded enormous power in financial circles, had a glamorous background in Hollywood filmmaking, and who held a series of high positions in Franklin Roosevelt's administration. And there was mother Rose, the lovely daughter of a storied mayor of Boston—stylish, reverent, eloquent in her own cool way—the ideal mother. The four sons seemed dashing and athletic, the five daughters pretty and competitive. The settings were usually Palm Beach or Cape Cod.

Politics was on the horizon. How could a fledgling picture magazine ask for more!

After the death of his older brother in World War II, the mantle fell to second son John. At first there were few if any indications to LIFE editors that he would become the most photographed person in the magazine's history. But from the decade that started so happily for the Kennedys in 1953, when John married the beautiful Jacqueline Lee Bouvier in Newport, and ended so tragically in Dallas, the Kennedys, in one fashion or another, were on LIFE's cover a record 21 times. And since then, the Kennedy story and its mystique have continued to occupy LIFE's cover—27 times in all (see pages 318-319). No wonder Teddy Kennedy asserted on the magazine's 50th anniversary that "LIFE has been the scrapbook for our family."

It is hard today to conjure up the excitement that most journalists felt covering J.F.K. It was a different time then, with seemingly limitless possibilities and expectations

In 1937 the whole Kennedy clan graced LIFE's pages for the first time. By this time Papa Joe had already befriended LIFE's owner and editor-in-chief, Henry Luce.

TIME/LIFE correspondent Hugh Sidey was Jack Kennedy's favorite reporter.

and a new and often naive set of rules. Hugh Sidey was a young reporter in the '50s working for LIFE in its Washington bureau. He later switched to LIFE's sister magazine, *Time,* but his allegiance and ties to the picture magazine remained strong and he kept on contributing Kennedy articles and insights to LIFE whenever he could. His enormously popular column "The Presidency" first ran in LIFE in April 1966 through 1972 and for the past 16 years has been a staple of *Time.* Considered Kennedy's favorite reporter, Hugh, today, five Presidents later, is a senior sage of the Washington scene and I have asked him to reach back in his memory and contribute to this introduction. Obligingly, Sidey begins:

"What was it about John Kennedy? I guess it was youth and a country that felt it was younger than it really was, and an old generation passing and still the sense that we had most of the world's wealth, power and brains. There was the whiff of romance and adventure, James Bond come alive with lovely parties and beautiful women and men and laughter and naughtiness and a cause that was as noble as any ever embraced by a politician.

"When covering Kennedy there was always the unexpected, the

sudden surge of sheer joy at hearing his eloquence, the belly laugh from his humor, the beauty of the settings that his family money could buy. He told me his favorite book was *Melbourne* and the picture of young English royalty that emerges from those pages is the pattern for his life—honor and duty pursued with joy and indulgence."

Sidey's first impression of Kennedy when he met him in a Senate elevator in 1957 was of a "sickly kid"; could this possibly be the guy, Sidey wondered, who almost became Adlai Stevenson's vice-presidential candidate the year before? But he showed instant warmth. "I suspect that came from meeting another reporter for LIFE," says Hugh. "He envisioned, quite correctly, many fine stories from the magazine on his way to the Oval Office, a journey, it turned out, he was already plotting."

The warmth was mutual. Sidey "plugged in," was given free range of the Senator's office and Robert Kennedy's basement quarters as the two starred in the dramatic Senate hearings on racketeering in organized labor, one as committee member, the other as counsel of that committee.

"Has there ever been a more succulent time for a young reporter? I doubt it. The mingling of journalism with power and wealth, now judged to have been a bad thing, was a new phenomenon in this country, or anywhere, and at least until it began to be corrupted years after Kennedy's death, it was a golden time for scribes. He talked to us, listened to us, honored us, ridiculed us, got angry at us, played with us, laughed with us, corrected us and all the time lifted our trade to new heights of respect and importance.

"Before long a few of us began to travel with Kennedy out to the primary states. The elite got to go with him on his private plane, the *Caroline.* It was a glimpse of the world that most of us had never seen. The interior of the plane was configured for kings, or their Ameri-

can equivalents. There was the lovely stewardess who rubbed Mr. French's special formula hair tonic into the Kennedy turf. He had fish chowder, his favorite food, by the barrel. What a way to go! Reporters and photographers were welcome almost anywhere he went. They could play with him, invade his bedroom when he was preparing for campaign stops, talk girls, sailboats or their craft with him. He had a curiosity as wide as the horizon. Kennedy was so trusting. I guess he had good right to be, with some of us at least. We never took him apart for his regal ways or his girls. We never had irrefutable evidence of the women and Kennedy was so much one of us nobody was going to cut him up for being rich, liking good food, good houses, sailboats."

During the summer of '60, when Kennedy was battling for and winning the Democratic candidacy, a new, young group of editors was taking over the leadership of LIFE. George Hunt, a tall, rugged, 42-year-old ex-Marine war hero was being named managing editor; the immediate deputies he chose were in their 30s. (I was one of them and at 32 was considered so young and untested by Time Inc.'s proprietor Henry Luce that the title of the job I was doing, assistant managing editor, was withheld for a full year.)

Even though the editorial page for the company—the place where each week Henry Luce made known his views on America and the world—ran in LIFE, *Time* had a long-standing reputation for editorializing in its news coverage, more often than not against Democrats. Hunt and his own new frontiersmen were concerned lest not only *Time* but their own magazine as well dim Jack Kennedy's chances, through a weekly page controlled by the very much Republican Luce. Whether to counter this possibility or not, it is fair to say that the Kennedy coverage that LIFE ran before the election of J.F.K. had the unmistakable look of a winner. One headline read 1960 PHENOMENON: ADORATION with pictures illustrating "the blissful fog of feminine adoration surrounding Jack Kennedy—the great phenomenon of the 1960 campaign."

Reporting the campaign for *Time*, it was difficult, too, for Sidey to remain impartial.

"The campaign was a rollick. I lost eight pounds covering Kennedy. We went from morning until night, always late, always packing in one more stop. When I switched to cover Nixon for a week, I gained it all back. That was sooo slow. Kennedy lost his voice, sucked his squares of toffee, practiced his breathing lessons. Kennedy would stop his caravan on country roads to buy apples, gab with a farmer. He'd slow down for nuns and kids, running three hours late. We'd chase after him 12 hours a day, then write most of the night trying to capture the rarity of this youthful crusade. What an adventure! Crowds in the sunlight on a Sunday in Cleveland, crowds on the campus of the University of Michigan, bigger crowds in frenzy in downtown New York, more crowds up in Harlem, peculiar crowds in Los Angeles, clean crowds in Idaho. People, people, people coming out to catch a glimpse of the young man with a cause."

Presidential candidate John Fitzgerald Kennedy and Henry Robinson Luce were no strangers; in fact they had been intimately connected for decades. In 1960 Kennedy sized Luce up in this way: "I like him. He is like a cricket, always chirping away. After all, he made a lot of money through his own individual enterprise so he naturally thinks that individual enterprise can do anything. I don't mind people like that. They have earned the right to talk that way . . . My father is the same way . . ."

With that remark Kennedy put his finger on a fortuitous similarity that had already assisted him throughout his political career and was about to give him, in a strange roundabout way, a final shove into the presidency itself. For Harry Luce, the opinionated, energetic, contro-

versial and brilliant proprietor of the enormously successful publishing empire spearheaded by *Time*, LIFE and *Fortune* magazines, and Joe Kennedy, the financier turned public servant who was masterminding his son's run for the presidency, were, in important ways, peas out of the same pod. Both cherished power. Both liked to be in control. Both had been mentioned at one time or another as presidential material. Both were self-made millionaires. Both had political prejudices, strong conservative inclinations and certain international blind spots. They were also close friends. They admired each other. Luce's son, Henry III, had even once worked for Kennedy as a personal assistant. The association went way back.

In 1937 Joe Kennedy had influence enough at Time Inc. to get a highly unfavorable *Fortune* cover story on him killed and replaced by a newly written, highly favorable one. The next year Luce and his new and famous wife, Clare Boothe, playwright, journalist and future Congresswoman, visited the Kennedys in England. Joe had recently been appointed ambassador to the Court of St. James's by President Roosevelt. Kennedy arranged for them to attend a ball given by the

Henry Luce and his wife Clare Boothe visited Joe Kennedy (right) on the French Riviera in 1956.

Jack and Jackie were warmly greeted by the Luces when they paid a visit to the new Time & Life Building in 1959.

Duchess of Sutherland and it was there that Luce was introduced to the Duke and Duchess of Windsor. Out of that meeting grew a relationship that led to the publishing of the Duke's memoirs in Luce's picture magazine in 1947, a journalistic coup that established LIFE's pages as *the* respectable and responsible place for the world's great to speak out, particularly about themselves. When Churchill followed, could Truman or MacArthur or Eisenhower or Tito or Khrushchev be far behind?

After a *Time* cover story on the Ambassador (his second; the first had appeared when Joe was Securities and Exchange commissioner—"an ideal policeman for the securities business") Luce and Kennedy met again in London with

LIFE author Teddy White—here with John F. Kennedy (center) and his aide Bill vanden Heuvel (left)—met with Mrs. Kennedy after the assassination and from this interview wrote the famous "Camelot" epilogue that gave this book its name.

Twenty-nine-year-old Paul Schutzer (pointing) never left the Democratic candidate's side during his run for the presidency. Many of his pictures of those exciting days are published here for the first time.

LIFE photographer Arthur Rickerby—seen receiving a White House photographers' award from the President—accompanied Kennedy to Texas in November of '63 and took some of the last pictures of him alive.

each trying to persuade the other that his views were correct—Luce urging that America join in a world effort against the Axis, the isolationist Kennedy all for appeasement.

"I must say that I was somewhat astonished at the kind of things that he would say to me," Luce recalled in a 1965 interview for the Oral History project of the Kennedy Library. "He thought that England was soon to be beaten. He put this in the most colorful language . . . my own feeling was that Hitler ought to be fought to the end, and that as much as possible the United States ought to join the fight."

After graduation from Harvard in 1940, young John Kennedy skillfully turned his senior thesis on Great Britain's unpreparedness for what obviously lay ahead into a publishable book. All Why England Slept needed to make it noticed was an introduction by a distinguished and responsible figure, and father Kennedy asked editor Luce over the transatlantic phone to do the honors.

"Well, send the manuscript and let me look at it," Luce replied. When the proofs arrived, Luce was pleased with what he read, especially with young John's emphasis

that blame had to be shared by all aspects of British opinion, with as much lack of foresight attributed to the Laborites as to the Conservatives. "What impressed me was, first, that he had done such a careful job of actually reviewing the facts," Luce remembered, "the facts such as attitudes and voting records, with regard to the crisis in Europe. And I was impressed with his careful scholarship, research, and also by his sense of personal involvement."

The introduction Luce wrote served him well, along with the push it gave the book. In likening Britain's mistakes and omissions to the ones he felt the Roosevelt administration was making, Luce could then needle his presidential candidate, Wendell Willkie, into being more forthright about the war clouds on the horizon. At the same time he could do a favor for his old friend in England. "I cannot recall a single man of my college generation," Luce waxed, "who could have written such an adult book on such a vitally important subject during his senior year in college . . . If John Kennedy is characteristic of the younger generation—and I believe he is—many of us would be happy to have the destinies of this Republic handed over to his generation at once."

Jack thought the introduction "wonderful" and wrote Luce to that effect, saying it made his book much more timely. "Especially is this true," his letter said, "of the point about the similarity of Chamberlain's 'Peace In Our Time,' and our 'We Will Never Fight in Foreign Wars' and the parallel effect that they have had on our war efforts. I missed this and it was very vital."

After publication, the youthful author visited Luce in his New York office, and a decade later, first as Congressman and then as Senator, he occasionally saw the editor he admired so much, but only casually. The relationship moved up another rung when John married Jackie, whose stepfather was an old Luce friend from Yale, classmate Hugh D. Auchincloss.

Joe Kennedy was a master at if not controlling, at least influencing, news events he cared about. One of his best friends was an esteemed columnist of the *New York Times*, Arthur Krock, who was instrumental in getting Kennedy's second book *Profiles in Courage* awarded the Pulitzer Prize. Many newsmen who did stories favorable to the Kennedys often found themselves on Joe's Christmas list.

Having discovered long before that Henry Luce was not for sale, at least Joe could stay very close to the man he considered to be the most influential in U.S. journalism. And especially close at crucial moments in the blossoming political life of his son. During the Democratic Convention of 1956, for instance, when John Kennedy made his almost successful run for the vice-presidential nomination on Adlai Stevenson's ticket, the Luces were guests of the Kennedys at their villa on the Riviera. After following the proceedings in Chicago by long distance with his friend, Luce cabled his editors from Europe that Jack was now "a considerable national figure" and they would be wise to give him "further treatment." In addition, the cable concluded, "We might be able to give strong mention to his best-selling book which *Time* did not, repeat not review."

"Further treatment" in the Luce publications followed and Jack Kennedy was usually outspokenly appreciative, even though he occasionally took a swipe at *Time* by claiming to prefer LIFE. "LIFE is the magazine," he once said. "That's the good one." He wrote to LIFE's editor "to let you know how much I appreciated the very fine story that appeared in LIFE Magazine a couple of weeks ago. You were exceedingly kind and I think LIFE provided me with the best pictures I will ever have of my daughter."

Late in 1957 Kennedy appeared on *Time's* cover for the first time because he seemed to be the front-running Democrat for the 1960 presidential nomination. A decade later, in a memo to Luce, *Time's* Marshall Berges, who had reported on Jack for the cover story, recalled Kennedy's reaction to it. "When the magazine appeared, Jack . . . called me in the middle of the night to register great pleasure . . . The expression of his pleasure went on for . . . perhaps 20 or 30 minutes; the sense of it was that the story would be enormously helpful to his career and that he would be grateful forever.

"Jack was so effusive," Berges continued, "that it made me uncomfortable . . . I was even more uncomfortable next day when Papa Joe called up to register his own joy with the story." He said 'Any time you need help, let me know.' Although I never did request help, he extended some anyway. Some three or four months later I became Detroit bureau chief, and Joe—on his own initiation—wrote to a number of his high-powered friends there, urging them to look after me and to lend assistance as I made my entrée into the community. And they did."

In 1960, on the very night Jack made his speech at the Democratic Convention in Los Angeles accepting his nomination for President, Joe Kennedy turned up at Luce's apartment in New York City on his way from Los Angeles to Europe. Luce recalled that he did think it a little odd that Kennedy had not remained in California to bask in the glow of his son's great achievement. It occurred to him, though, that the reason for this unexpected visit was, partly at least, to seek support from Luce's normally Republican magazines in the difficult campaign ahead. Luce remembered the evening:

"When we adjourned to the living room after dinner, Joe still showed no signs of getting down to business. So I opened up. I said my attitude (as editor-in-chief of Time Inc. publications) toward Jack could be very simply stated. Let us divide the question into two parts: domestic policy, foreign policy.

"As for the domestic policy, naturally it was to be assumed that Jack would adopt a 'liberal' policy. Old Joe broke in with blazing blue eyes and many a goddamn. He said, 'Harry, you know goddamn well no son of mine could ever be a goddamn liberal.'

"I told Joe to hush. It was the nature of American politics that in order to win, a Democratic candidate for the presidency had to take a liberal position (while, of course, retaining the automatic support of the solid South) and that he would not hold that against him.

"'But,' I said, 'if Jack shows any signs of going soft on Communism [in foreign policy]—then we would clobber him.'

"Joe said, 'Well, you don't have to worry about that.'

"There wasn't much more to say as we waited . . . Then the TV came on and there was John Fitzgerald Kennedy with voice and gesture and face and figure that would soon become imperishable in the world's vision.

"What must have been the emotions of that father watching and listening to that son?

"When the speech was done, we chatted for a while, and then Joe got up to leave. At the doorway, he turned to me, took my hand and said, 'I want you to know that we are truly grateful for all that you have done for Jack.'

"It was a moment after the door had closed before my inner ear took in these words. I was touched, of course, but what had I done? Had I ever done too much?"

Even though Luce admitted afterward that Time Inc. was all along going to be for Richard Nixon no matter what, there was much speculation in the press at the time that this might be the election when Luce would finally switch his allegiance from the Republican Party and opt for his friend's son, whom he so greatly admired. During the summer of '60 the Democratic candidate, hoping for this kind of endorsement, lunched with Luce and his top editors in the board room of the Time & Life Building in New York City. The luncheon

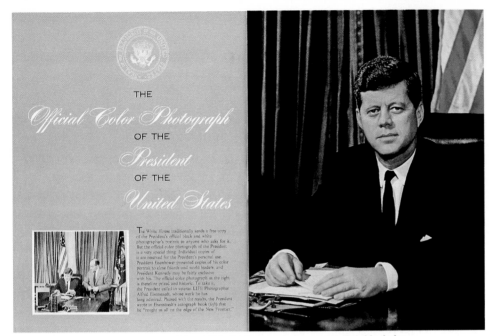

THE
Official Color Photograph
OF THE
President
OF THE
United States

The White House traditionally sends a free copy of the President's official black and white photographer's portrait to anyone who asks for it. But the official color photograph of the President is a very special thing. Individual copies of it are reserved for the President's personal use. President Eisenhower presented copies of his color portrait to close friends and world leaders, and President Kennedy may be fairly exclusive with his. The official color photograph at the right is therefore prized and historic. To take it, the President called in veteran LIFE Photographer Alfred Eisenstaedt, whose work he has long admired. Pleased with the results, the President wrote in Eisenstaedt's autograph book (*left*) that he "caught us all on the edge of the New Frontier."

Alfred Eisenstaedt, the dean of the LIFE photographers, was asked to take Kennedy's official presidential pictures, first in black and white, then in color.

meeting was a real success and Kennedy's appeal was felt by all. When the candidate wrote to thank Luce, he mentioned in the letter Luce's recent agreement to write a revised forward to a new edition of *Why England Slept*. "While I have a faint feeling that your 1960 endorsement of the book may be the last one I shall get—nevertheless you were very generous at the luncheon, and made it a happy two hours." J.F.K. had got the message.

By September, two months before election day, Time Inc.'s top editors were giving Kennedy the edge in "eloquence," "grace," "style" and "aggressiveness." Against him were his "cynical over-promises" and his "remote" temperament. When the votes from the editors that counted were in, except for one senior man on *Time*, Nixon got the nod. Of course that was Luce's inclination all along. Nixon was "a man of broader sympathies, more responsible, more judicious."

In mid-October, only a few weeks before voting day, a two-part editorial in LIFE stated the verdict. Editorial No. 1 dealt with domestic issues and said on this score "LIFE believes that Nixon would make a much better President than Kennedy ... [who] sees national progress not as the achievement of

a free people, but as 'the big assignment, the big task, the big function of the federal government.' " It went on to ask "How did able Jack Kennedy ever get entangled with this drive toward statism? A bold youthful vision of power, his country's as well as his own, is part of the reason. But a clearer explanation is his fascination with the mechanics of power in the Democratic party ..."

In editorial No. 2 the following week LIFE admitted right off that "the difference between the two candidates on world policy is narrow and the choice is not easy. Both men are young, confident, patriotic and full of fresh ideas and serious purpose ..." The editorial presented almost no evidence of Nixon's superiority except that the experienced Henry Cabot Lodge, long a Luce friend and a former employee as well, was also on the ticket. "With Nixon and Lodge in charge of U.S. world policy we shall feel both safer and more hopeful in the enlarging struggle ..."

A rather lukewarm endorsement, to be sure. Nor did Luce think Nixon was going to win. He was already scribbling notes for stories on a Kennedy administration, the prospect of which he found exciting indeed. Helping Kennedy in the forthcoming election was *Time's* suddenly scrupulously fair reporting on the heated campaign and TV

debates between the candidates. Luce hadn't ordered it but he was delighted by the impartiality. He had been able to make his usual Republican endorsement without alienating conservatives or violating his deepest political convictions, while at the same time the fair and favorable reporting was helping his sentimental favorite eke out the slimmest of victories. Harry was eating his cake and having it too.

The easygoing, slap-on-the-back relationship between Kennedy and members of the press who had followed him so closely during the campaign came to an abrupt end after the voting results were in. Sidey continues to recall those heady days:

"It changed when he became President, a force that could not rightly be defined but could be felt. We kept our distance. We debated whether to call him Mr. President or Senator and decided on the latter, but he really had the power. The presidential apparatus began to gather around him. Secret Service, Signal Corps, Air Force, transition. John Kennedy drifted off just beyond reach. He would still be more accessible, far more informal than any modern President but he would be wary and watch his words, which were now all freighted with explosives. Still, the spirit stayed."

Back in New York the editors of LIFE unloosed just about every photographer we could lay our hands on to cover the Inauguration. We were bedazzled by the spectacle: the white-skirted, ice-cold Capitol standing at attention for this coronation, the entertainers, the high hats, the festive parade, the balls, the dignitaries, the music, the huge Kennedy family, the stunning Jackie, and especially our new young President and his bold beautiful words.

Again Luce was in the midst of intimate Kennedy affairs. First—his son, Henry Luce III, recalled—Jack submitted a draft of his Inaugural address to him for suggestions. Luce told him that he should insert the word "God," which was otherwise missing, which he did. Then, Harry and Clare were included in the Kennedy inner circle, riding on their special bus to the gala while Teddy led everyone in song, and then sitting in the Kennedy box at the Inaugural ball.

From the LIFE coverage hundreds of rolls of film were carried up from Washington and quickly developed and printed. The prints piled up on our layout tables, each one better than the last. We did our story for the magazine but there were too many wonderful pictures so we decided to put out an Inauguration "special" as well. We put it together and wrote it practically overnight and it was on the newsstands in a couple of days. Back in Washington Sidey was feeling the same excitement as this new era unfolded.

"There began the next morning after the Inauguration what surely must be the golden age of journalism. We were off. Pencils at the ready. Cameras having increased manyfold, TV now beginning to understand that the young ruler was hot footage. The ruckuses at Hickory Hill where Bobby Kennedy lived were now better news than congressional hearings. Kennedy's clothes rocked the fashion industry. What he ate inspired chefs the world over. Jackie's styles made and broke the impresarios of Seventh Avenue.

"Merriman Smith, dean of the White House press correspondents, was appalled. He was used to the structured and easy life around F.D.R. and Truman and Ike, remote and godly figures who did not cavort with the common reporters

and took things rather easy. The *New York Times'* venerable Scotty Reston called on the President and suggested that he should set up some dignified and responsible contacts with the media and when he had important things to say he should say them in the *New York Times,* which would treat them as they should be treated. The President, Reston hinted, would only get into trouble if he talked to others. Kennedy responded that he had a lot of friends in the press corps and he had managed pretty well up to then. He would talk with whom he wanted and when he wanted. Reston never really recovered from that, he never quite accepted Kennedy as a legitimate President."

It has often been said that *Time* magazine makes enemies while LIFE makes friends; it is something inherent in the nature of the beasts—the different kinds of minds at work on the two magazines and of course their different roles and approaches. *Time,* Kennedy thought, began treating him like an adversary instead of a friend. Often criticized (he felt unjustly), Kennedy complained bitterly not only to Sidey and other *Time* correspondents on the scene but to Luce as well. Sidey found the President's attention to what was written about him flattering, though at times unnerving. "He called me up one

night after an exhausting week, and just as I was mixing my first martini, he launched into a tirade about how we had some story wrong. He must have been eating. I could hear the smack of his jowls as he talked."

As time went on the President got more and more thin-skinned and testy over press criticism, *Time's* in particular. He had arranged with Luce to have a copy of the magazine delivered to him straight from the printing plant every Sunday night, before it was available to the public or even to the Time-Life Washington correspondents Monday morning. He could tell by name what editor was top editing; when the style of the National Affairs section changed, even slightly, he knew who was responsible. When he detected a Republican bias, Kennedy would grumble that *Time* was run by overpaid editors who lived in posh Greenwich, Connecticut estates, ate at "21" and knew little of the world.

More than once Kennedy phoned the Time-Life Washington bureau on a Friday night when the magazine was ready to close, asking, "What are you bastards going to do to me *next* week?" In the summer of 1961 he had Ted Sorensen and staff prepare a detailed memorandum an-

The cover of the Dec. 19, 1960, issue of LIFE showed the President-elect, his wife and John Jr. at the baby's christening. Prophetically, inside was the story of the opening of Lerner and Loewe's Broadway musical _Camelot_, photographed for LIFE by Milton Greene. Kennedy had been enamored of the Knights of the Round Table legend since childhood. The play, and especially its title song, soon became his favorite. Richard Burton's rugged yet tender King Arthur and Julie Andrews' glowing Guinevere seemed to many to resemble the young couple about to assume the American throne.

alyzing and comparing *Time's* treatment of President Eisenhower and himself during their first six months in office.

The 24-page report listed scores of statements that had been favorable to Ike and just as many undercutting Kennedy. "The technique," the report concluded, "is that of *Time* supplying a meaningful, acceptable, positive interpretation whenever an Eisenhower . . . statement was vague and possibly contradictory . . . The Kennedy report is not all bad. There are occasional words of praise, but there are mostly cynical comments, criticism and doubt. There are no benefits of the doubt given, no excuses or rationalizations, no hopeful words or acceptable interpretations. In contrast the picture is dark indeed."

Luce had long ago withdrawn from active editing and the men he chose to run his magazines were strong-minded individualists with politics and prejudices of their own. On broad policy the Proprietor was still active, but on week to week coverage he was leery to interfere, keeping for the most part very much out of his editors' hair. Even so, sometimes Luce felt the wrath of the President in person. Wrath it was, but dished out politely as well as sharply, for Jack Kennedy still addressed his father's friend as Mr. Luce and still looked upon him with considerable awe. Once Sidey found himself awkwardly caught in the middle between these two powerful men.

"It occurred during one of Kennedy's fits about the magazine. Luce came down to talk it over and went into the Oval Office. When the two men emerged, Luce looked shaken and Kennedy looked pleased. 'Ask him,' Kennedy suddenly said. 'Sidey here is a fair reporter. Ask him if you treat me fairly. If you went out on Pennsylvania Avenue and asked the average man there, is *Time* fair to the President, what would he say?' I stood there absolutely appalled that Kennedy would do that to his old pal. Here I am standing between my boss and the President of the United States and asked to render a judgment that either way will ruin me. Suddenly God intervened. 'The President's right, Mr. Luce,' I said. 'If I went out on the Avenue and asked the average person he would say that *Time* was unfair to the President. But the fact is that three out of every four of those people are dyed-in-the-wool Democrats and they would say anything we printed was unfair to the President. Washington is a Democratic town!' I saw Kennedy get a disgusted look on his face but not without some admiration. Luce brightened. 'That's right,' he said. 'Down in Phoenix where I've spent the winter they would not say that.' My job was safe another few days."

After one particular drubbing by the President, Luce asked his aide Bill Furth to make a study of whether *Time's* editors really did have it in for Kennedy. *Time's* misdeeds, as Kennedy listed them to the Washington bureau, included repeatedly ticking off his failures and neglecting his accomplishments, portraying him over and over again as "weak and failing," trying whenever possible to "destroy me . . . make it as tough for me as possible . . . see that I fail . . . get me." After careful study, Furth determined that the magazine sometimes "went beyond criticism and into nagging and harping" and was "overlong on the President's failures, possibly to the point of distorted perspective." Furth's conclusion was that "*Time's* emphatic journalism sometimes becomes overemphatic."

As for LIFE, except for some editorials that the President thought were dead wrong and that outraged him, the relations were warm. LIFE had been not only fair but friendly in its campaign coverage, and no less than ecstatic over the Inauguration. During the years that followed, LIFE's Kennedy stories were almost always complimentary. Sidey himself wrote many of them, including a fascinating piece on Kennedy's reading habits and tastes and a fine story about Jackie and the wonders she accomplished refurbishing the White House. Jackie shot a few pictures for the magazine and the President wrote several articles. His official picture was shot by the dean of LIFE's photographers, Alfred Eisenstaedt. Pictures were the key, of course. Most of LIFE's stories were told through photographs and it was pretty hard to take a bad one of the Kennedy family.

Along with the constant intellectual ferment, Sidey found the Kennedy years filled with an aura of romance:

"I doubt if many reporters would put it in those terms. But that was just what it was. Kennedy wanted to ride with the gods and I believe he did a bit. Partly, because of the sweep of his view, he refined the presidential junket. He loved to travel. He relished Air Force One. Nothing pleased him more than to unveil another foreign adventure unless it was actually climbing aboard the big bird and heading out for Ireland, Germany, Vienna. The smell of adventure was in the air. He was Marlborough going to the Continent, he was Teddy Roosevelt in the Canal.

"Flying home from the Vienna meeting with Khrushchev, Kennedy called me up to his cabin and there he was in his shorts, the Navy corpsmen working over his back. He looked half dead. He wanted to know what we were going to write. He was grim and discouraged.

"In Palm Beach two nights later, what a contrast! Frank Sinatra records wafted the crooner's voice out over the elegant patio. There were daiquiris for the few guests. Kennedy was the rich boy once again, in soft shoes, cream slacks and polo shirt. He laughed about de Gaulle and Khrushchev and the contrast, marveled at the brutal eyes of the Soviet boss. Though he had been humbled, he was not contrite or frightened. He had that inner confidence still, which kept suggesting to all of us that he was just trying to sort out events, get in his crouch and go hard at it again. That is an appealing characteristic. Kennedy was a fighter.

"And there was something else—there was accumulating wisdom. That is the combination of experience and intelligence, rather a rare quality. I had the feeling in writing about Kennedy in those last months that he knew the jungle through which he walked and he knew the habits of the animals. He was cautious, but he was bold. Vietnam never would have happened as it did had Kennedy lived. The world would have been far different had he not been murdered. We had a man whom we could admire, one who could surprise us and inspire us. There is no better story for a journalist."

And then, suddenly, on an autumn Friday, it was over. A few of the top editors of LIFE were halfway through lunch with Henry Luce in a private dining room on the 47th floor of the Time & Life Building. Normally, I would have been among them but November of 1963 found me in Japan researching a special issue on that exotic, re-emerging land. I was asleep in the Tarawaya Inn in Kyoto. It was still dark when a hand shook my shoulder and an urgent voice kept telling me something in Japanese. All I could understand was the word Kennedy over and over but I instantly knew that something terrible had happened to him. Two associates and I huddled around a little transistor radio on which we had found an English-speaking station. I had never felt so far away from home. All day long wherever we went the Japanese people would bow to us and say how sorry they were. Even in Hiroshima two days later citizens showed us their respect. As America united that weekend and became one enormous entity watching and waiting for the staggering tragedy to play itself out, I was 7,000 miles away, grasping at scraps of news, a part of none of it, told to stay there and stick it out, frustrated and sad and angry.

Back home, my associates were doing extraordinary things. One of them was Dick Stolley, the Los Angeles bureau chief of LIFE. Dick was sitting in his office in Beverly Hills when his close friend and co-correspondent Tommy Thompson yelled from the A.P. ticker machine, "Dick, Kennedy has been shot in Dallas." Everybody in the office ran for the machine, crowded around it and just watched the keys pound out more and more hideous details. In less than an hour Stolley and Thompson and two photographers were on a plane for Dallas. At first they would be the only two LIFE correspondents on the scene; the photographers would reinforce staffer Arthur Rickerby who had been traveling with the President and might even have taken pictures of the assassination. No such luck, Stolley soon found out; the news photographers were traveling in a car well behind Kennedy's and were out of sight of the presidential car when Oswald fired the shots.

Once in Dallas, Thompson headed off to see what he could do on the Oswald end of the story. The results of his efforts were astounding; he not only found Oswald's wife and family and persuaded them to talk but also hid them away from the rest of the press to protect the exclusivity of his story.

For his part, Stolley began plugging into local sources. It was not long before a Dallas stringer weighed in with some startling information she had got from the police: somebody had taken an 8mm color film of the entire assassination. Stolley finally found that the someone was a local garment manufacturer named Abraham Zapruder but no one answered the phone listed under that name. Stolley called every 15 minutes until 9 o'clock that night when finally an emotion-pinched voice answered. When Zapruder heard that the caller was from LIFE, his voice immediately became more cordial and re-

Dick Stolley and Tommy Thompson of LIFE's Los Angeles bureau teamed up to produce some of the historic coverage of the Kennedy assassination. Stolley tracked down the only film of the shooting and acquired it exclusively for LIFE. Thompson found the assassin's wife and mother and interviewed them ahead of the authorities. The picture below was taken in the hotel room where Thompson hid the Oswald family from the rest of the press. Marina Oswald is at right and Thompson can be seen reflected in the dresser mirror at far right, just above Oswald's mother.

ceptive. Yes, he had taken the pictures. In fact, he had seen the developed film already. No, Stolley could not come out to his house right then. He was too tired, too upset that night. But yes, Stolley could meet him at his office at 9 o'clock the next morning.

Dick was there at 8:00, along with a Secret Service detail. In a tiny room LIFE magazine and the Secret Service were shown the most historic frames of home-movie film ever taken.

"I'll never forget that as long as I live," says Dick today. "The only sound in the room was the creaking of this old 8mm Bell & Howell projector. You see the motorcade coming around the corner, the President's hands going up to his throat, you see Mrs. Kennedy turning to him, smiling, then suddenly realizing something terrible is happening. You get to frame 313, that awful frame when the top of the President's head simply disappears."

Zapruder ran the film over and over as Stolley's mind reeled and his heart beat faster and faster. He knew LIFE had to have this film at any price. The next hour, he knew, would test his powers of persuasion to the limit. He had to do everything just right.

By the time the screening ended, other reporters were in the hallway, clamoring to see the film the cops had told them about, calling to see Mr. Zapruder. Zapruder told them he was honor-bound to talk to Stolley first. "They kept pleading with him," Stolley remembers, "and their faces were stricken." Stolley wondered whether or not this garment manufacturer knew the value of what he had. He mentioned several figures and the two finally agreed upon $50,000—for print rights. But it was not the money that won the day, it was LIFE's reputation. Zapruder had already had a nightmare that the film had fallen into the wrong hands and was being shown in sleazy joints on 42nd Street in New York City.

Stolley typed out a little contract on Zapruder's typewriter and both men signed. Then he ducked out a back door and Zapruder stepped out of his office into the corridor and told the angry mob of network, newspaper and magazine representatives that the film had been sold to LIFE and was on its way to New York. (LIFE sewed up all rights the next day by an additional payment of $100,000. Zapruder's faith in LIFE was vindicated. The film, made available to the Warren Commission, proved to be the only evidence the investigating team had of the moment of impact. After its official use the magazine returned the original film, in 1975, to Zapruder's heirs, who donated it to the National Archives but who retain television rights.)

Tommy Thompson's coup of finding Maria Oswald stands high on the list of great LIFE interviews. So does Theodore H. White's post-funeral discussion with Jacqueline Kennedy. When it ran in the magazine along with the pictures of that majestic funeral march to Arlington, it moved a nation and gave the Kennedy reign a name: Camelot. In a TV interview 23 years later—just a few days before his own death—for an ABC special on LIFE's 50th birthday, White spoke of his role in the magazine's coverage of Kennedy's assassination.

"I was having lunch with an old friend (and assistant publisher of LIFE), Jim Shepley, on the top floor of the building. And the waiter tapped him and said, 'Mr. Shepley, the President's been shot' ... We left our forks on the table and headed for the elevator, got to the 29th floor and on the way down, Jim was saying, 'We have to stop the press.' LIFE went to press on Wednesday night and by Friday afternoon two and a half million covers had already been printed. At a cost of more than a million dollars they were scrapped and the magazine was opened up for assassination coverage. And I said, 'That's my story, Jim, I'm going.' George Hunt was editor. I got cash from everybody in the room, grabbed a cab, was on my way to La Guardia when the radio said he's being flown to Washington. Got into Washington on the shuttle, used up all the cash to get a car to Andrews Air Force Base and saw Kennedy arrive.

"Now that was late Friday ... and so all day Saturday I was with the ceremonies. Saw the family ... and I remember sitting there in Ave Harriman's house where I'd found lodging. And crying and drinking and typing and writing the first story about the preparations for the funeral, which I must have got off to them by, oh, 3 o'clock Sunday morning, at which time they started rolling the press ... The next episode was more hairy because Friday, one week after the assassination, Mrs. Kennedy suddenly telephoned to my house in New York. It was almost an unreal conversation. She felt the American people were going to forget John F. Kennedy ... And she wanted me to come because she had a message to give the American people. Remember it was Friday night, so we stopped the press for a second time ... Mrs. Kennedy wanted to be out of the camera and television and be with a friend and just talk her heart out because she loved him—and I must confess I loved him, too."

White drove through a hurricane and arrived at Hyannis Port in the middle of the night to be greeted by his pale and sad friend.

"She told me so many things that I realized should not be printed at that time. But one thing stood out. She said that when Jack quoted lyrics they were usually classical. But, she said, 'At night, before we'd go to sleep, Jack liked to play records, and the song he loved most came at the end of this record, and the lines he loved to hear were:

Don't let it be forgot
That once there was a spot
For one brief shining moment that
was known as Camelot

" 'This was Camelot, Teddy,' she told me. 'Let's not forget the time of Camelot.' She told me about the assassination, the bullets in the sun and the shattering of his skull . . . I was trying to soothe her at the same time wondering what I could write for LIFE. And finally after she was settled down—it was an extremely emotional ordeal for her—I sat down to write the story again. And there again you go through your notes and you cry and about 4 o'clock on Saturday morning . . . knowing the presses are waiting . . . and knowing the thing has to run and you can't have a day off to write the story, you have to do it right now. I used the telephone in her kitchen . . . and rambled off the Camelot story, which later on became a signature for the whole Kennedy era."

In the same TV interview Teddy White summed up his feelings about Kennedy as a President. "I felt . . . that he was a key figure of the 20th century . . . He was the first Catholic to be elected President, an Irish Catholic. It meant that all the other subdued ethnics who hadn't yet seized the opportunities of American politics would follow after him . . . He opened the gates for all the new surges in American life, surges in American culture. He came down hard on the environmental thing very early. He got the test-ban treaty through. He did remarkable things in three short years. And he left his work unfinished . . . He was cut off just as things were about to come to harvest . . . If he had gone on till 1968 it might have been . . . one of the three most memorable administrations in American history."

John Kennedy's mind fascinated the world. In LIFE in the first of a series of articles taken from Arthur Schlesinger's book *A Thousand Days*, the Pulitzer Prize-winning historian who had resigned from Harvard to serve as a special assistant to the President, summed up that remarkable mind.

"He was a man of action who could pass over to the realm of ideas with perfect ease and confidence. His mind was not prophetic, impassioned, mystical, utopian or ideological. It was less exuberant than Theodore Roosevelt's, less scholarly than Wilson's, less adventurous than Franklin Roosevelt's. But it had its own salient qualities—it was roving, direct, open, independent, impatient, objective, critical, practical, ironic, skeptical, unfettered and insatiable."

Adding to the aura of his administration was J.F.K.'s love of poetry. Ever since he was a child, Kennedy had been drawn to verse. Now poetry decorated and flavored the Kennedy tenure. He asked Robert Frost to read a poem at his Inauguration. The poet, complying, introduced his work with a salute to "A Golden Age of poetry and power of which this noonday's the beginning hour."

He kept anthologies of poetry in his sitting room and read aloud to Jackie, who in turn could quote his favorite poems and did so often. One of them was Alan Seeger's "I Have a Rendezvous with Death":

It may be he shall take my hand
And lead me into his dark lane
And close my eyes and quench my breath . . .
But I've a rendezvous with Death.

J.F.K. taught couplets to young Caroline. One that she learned by heart, by Edna St. Vincent Millay, he used spontaneously to introduce a visiting group to the White House.

Safe upon the solid rock the ugly houses stand:
Come and see my shining palace built upon the sand!

Referring to himself and his critics, he recited a Robert Graves translation of a poem by bullfighter Domingo Ortega:

Bullfight critics ranked in rows
Crowd the enormous Plaza full;
But only one is there who knows
And he's the man that fights
the bull.

A passage from Shakespeare's *Henry V*—a speech given by the King to his knights on the eve of battle—was another of Kennedy's favorites. J.F.K. thought the poem summed up what he and his closest associates were feeling.

. . . We shall be remembered—
We few, we happy few, we band of brothers . . .
And Gentlemen . . . now abed
Shall think themselves accurs'd
they were not here.

J.F.K.'s love of poetry inspired others to use verse on official occasions. The Irish ambassador presented a cup for young John's christening with a poem that the President wished had been said for him:

. . . When the storms break for him
May the trees shake for him
Their blossoms down;
And in the night that he is troubled
May a friend wake for him
So that his time be doubled;
And at the end of all loving
and love
May the man above
Give him a crown.

And witness the scene six months after his murder when, at the Democratic National Convention that had just chosen a Johnson-Humphrey ticket, tough little Bobby Kennedy rose to introduce a film honoring his brother. For 16 minutes he was not allowed to speak by the stampede of applause. When he finally did, he softly quoted from *Romeo and Juliet:*

When he shall die,
Take him and cut him out in little stars,
And he will make the face of heaven so fine,
That all the world will be in love with night,
And pay no worship to the garish sun.

No wonder Jacqueline Kennedy, in her great sorrow, wished to have the time just passed, a time of poetry and power, remembered as Camelot.

Chapter 1

THE PROUD AND PRIVILEGED CLAN

John Fitzgerald Kennedy was born on May 29, 1917, two months after the U.S. had entered World War I. The pristine master bedroom of the wood frame house in quiet, suburban Brookline little resembled the squalid tenement rooms in Boston that sheltered the births of some of his Irish-spawned forebears two generations before. In the years from 1845 to 1855 more than a million Irish had fled the old country, leaving behind the tyrannical oppression of English landlords and a potato blight that brought mass starvation. Twenty dollars was the cost of a ticket aboard rickety freighters—"coffin ships"—for the six-week voyage to Boston. In one year alone more than 30,000 of the 100,000 who attempted the voyage died en route. Once in America, the survivors met a new oppression: a racial and religious prejudice as harsh on the part of the Yankees as the Irish had encountered under the English. Shut out of the professions and "polite" society, the Irish kept their own company in their waterfront slums while improving their principal skill—politics. From 1885 onward they ruled Boston. One of their mayors was an archetypical politician named John F. Fitzgerald. Another influential politician and an affluent businessman as well was Patrick J. Kennedy. When the daughter of one and the son of the other were joined in wedlock and produced a son of their own who would one day become the President of the United States, it was clear that "Honey Fitz" and "P.J." had founded a clan that was to fulfill all those immigrant dreams.

The second child of Joe and Rose Kennedy, John, shown here at nine, grew up very much in the shadow of his older brother, Joe, who could do no wrong in his parents' eyes. Jack, as he came to be called, was a sickly, shy child with little to distinguish him other than a quick intellect and a power to charm.

The tenement apartment on Ferry Street where John Fitzgerald began his life had two rooms no bigger than large closets. A water closet served not only the 37 residents of the cramped dwelling but the customers of the tavern below as well. Deciding early not to follow in his father's footsteps as a fish peddler, John was determined to excel in everything he did, becoming, even though he was small, a champion runner, swimmer and soccer player. He drove his mind, too, graduating from the difficult Boston Latin School and being accepted by the Harvard Medical School without a college degree. But when his father died during his first year there and money was needed, politics beckoned, leading to a career not only as a U.S. Congressman but all the way to mayor of Boston. Honey Fitz they called him for the sweet, silken sheen of his blarney—and for some grocery-store sugar he had swiped as a kid. The light of Honey Fitz's life was his daughter Rose, whom he schooled at convents, and showed off to the public by squiring the young beauty about town.

"Dad persuaded us to work hard at whatever we did. We soon learned that competition in the family was a kind of dry run for the world outside. At the same time, everything channeled into public service. There just wasn't any point in going into business."

As a boy Patrick J. Kennedy worked on the Boston docks, loading and unloading cargo and later, with his savings, he bought a small tavern on Haymarket Square. Shrewd, well organized, with one eye always on the future, P.J. established his own business importing liquor, then branched out into politics, serving eight terms in the state legislature before becoming the powerful yet kindly boss of his local Boston ward. The light of P.J.'s life was his handsome, headstrong son Joe, whom he sent to Boston Latin and Harvard to ready himself for the world.

The lights of their lives were married 19 years after this picture was taken showing Honey Fitz and P.J. vacationing in Asheville, North Carolina.

Rose holds baby Rosemary who is flanked by Jack on the right and everybody's favorite—first-born Joe Jr. A slow, taciturn child, Rosemary turned out to be retarded, a fact the Kennedys tried their hardest to disguise.

A month before the wedding Joe bought this clapboard house on Beals Street in the Boston suburb of Brookline and it was here that John Fitzgerald Kennedy was born. Years later, long after the growing Kennedy family had moved away to more capacious quarters, volunteer workmen were refurbishing the house as befitted the birthplace of a President.

The birth of America's most spectacular family

ose was five and Joe seven hen they first met at a oint family outing at Old Orchard each in Maine. It was there that ey re-met 11 years later and ell in love. The romance lossomed during Joe's years at arvard. Honey Fitz opposed their arriage until the shrewd, ersistent suitor of his daughter as hailed as the youngest bank resident ever in the state. lthough the belle of Irish ociety had entertained 450 uests at her debutante party, her edding was a simple affair erformed by a cardinal in his rivate chapel.

With unerring skill he ruthlessly built a $500 million fortune.

Joe Jr. (left was bigger, 22 months older, more outgoing and tougher than John. He seemed destined not only for politics but in the minds of his family for the presidency some day. In childhood fights, Joe often thrashed his younger brother but John never resented him.

Big businessmen are the most overrated men in the country," Joe Kennedy once observed to his oldest sons. "Here I am, a boy from East Boston, and I took 'em. So don't be impressed."

Joe Kennedy's capitalistic gifts were visible early. While he was still an undergraduate, he and another student bought a bus and operated sight-seeing tours in Boston. He spent a restive 18 months after college as a state bank examiner, then parlayed his father's connections and his own business acumen into the presidency of a small bank. He was 25.

Banking shortly led to other profitable ventures, in real estate and the stock market, and, in the late 1920s, to his first big fortune—in the infant movie business. One of the few speculators to anticipate the crash of 1929, he managed to bail out early. In the frenzied maneuvering after the crash, Kennedy grew richer still through his role in a "pool" that artificially manipulated a stock's price through calculated rumors and trading. A short time later, as

the first chairman of the Securities and Exchange Commission, he enforced federal regulations against the very practice he had engaged in. He had also cashed in on the national thirst. Before the repeal of the Prohibition Amendment, he became the U.S. distributor of several British distillers and imported thousands of cases of liquor under "medicinal" licenses issued in Washington. When repeal became law, he was ready. At the 20th reunion of his Harvard class, he listed his profession as "capitalist."

A Democrat more because of his heritage than because of his philosophy, he entered politics as an enthusiastic Roosevelt booster in 1932. Through F.D.R.'s first two terms he took on one tough government job after another, including the U.S. ambassadorship to the Court of St. James's. "Well, Rose," he commented to his wife as they dressed for dinner with the King and Queen, "this is a helluva long way from East Boston, isn't it?"

His isolationist views made him a controversial ambassador during his tenure. A year after re-

turning home he consistently predicted the defeat of the Allies and opposed U.S. intervention up to the attack on Pearl Harbor.

Back in private business, he was a bigger smash than ever. He turned to real estate, buying large chunks of property in mid-Manhattan and elsewhere and selling them at enormous profit. His most monumental deal was the 1945 purchase of the Merchandise Mart in Chicago for $13 million. The Mart, valued at $35 million in 1964, now earns twice its original purchase price in annual rental payments.

Even though his fortune grew to half a billion dollars, it was not primarily money he was after. It was power and social position, and money was the only way he could get them.

Boldly taken and cleverly augmented, the Kennedy millions served their purpose—as prelude. Joe Kennedy's first and last concern was best summed up by an old friend from Boston. "He's sort of like a caterpillar; he couldn't quite become a butterfly, but his boys were going to fly no matter what."

All business in the office, all family man at home, Joe Kennedy had few of the virtues or principles of his father, who on his deathbed burned thousands of IOUs he had collected over the years from loans to anybody in need.

"The U.S.A.'s Nine-Child Envoy" one British newspaper called Joe when he turned up for his new job as ambassador to the Court of St. James's. Here father, mother and five of the brood lined up for cameramen in the yard of the ambassadorial residence.

Eleven ambassadors for the price of one

Arriving in England in early 1938, Ambassador Kennedy was graduated into a social climate from which his family had always been excluded in his native Boston. For his presentation at Court, Joe refused to wear the traditional knee breeches and silk stockings.

At their first day at London's Gibbs School, Bobby, 13, and Teddy, 6 (both at left), were challenged to a fight by British classmates.

John and Bobby got a foretaste of public life as they watched a parade from the London embassy.

eefeater gave Bobby d Teddy and Jean and a uple of older friends a ur of the Tower of London.

Teddy got some friendly advice about picture taking as he and sister Jean watched the changing of the guard at Buckingham Palace.

Kathleen Kennedy went to the Cambridge University steeplechase with her future husband the Marquess of Hartington.

Back home Joe Jr. got a banged head playing against a visiting British Rugby team that thrashed Harvard 50-0.

A happy 1939 lineup gave no hint of the many family tragedies that lay ahead

This striking picture of the new ambassador to the Court of St. James's and his jubilant family speaks nothing but success. But future triumphs would be tempered by bitter tragedy. The scorecard for Joe and Rose's brood today: (from left to right) Eunice (married to Sargent Shriver); John, murdered by an assassin; Rosemary, a

victim of prefrontal lobotomy; Jean (married to Stephen
Smith); Teddy, tainted by Chappaquiddick and divorced; Joe Jr.,
killed in aircraft explosion during World War II; Pat (divorced
from the late Peter Lawford); Bobby, murdered by an assassin;
Kathleen, widowed in World War II before dying in plane crash.

Between bouts with sickness and pain, J.F.K. lived fast and hard

Always an enormou success with the ladie and one of the mos eligible bachelor anywhere, Jacl enjoyed himself at the Stork Club in 1948

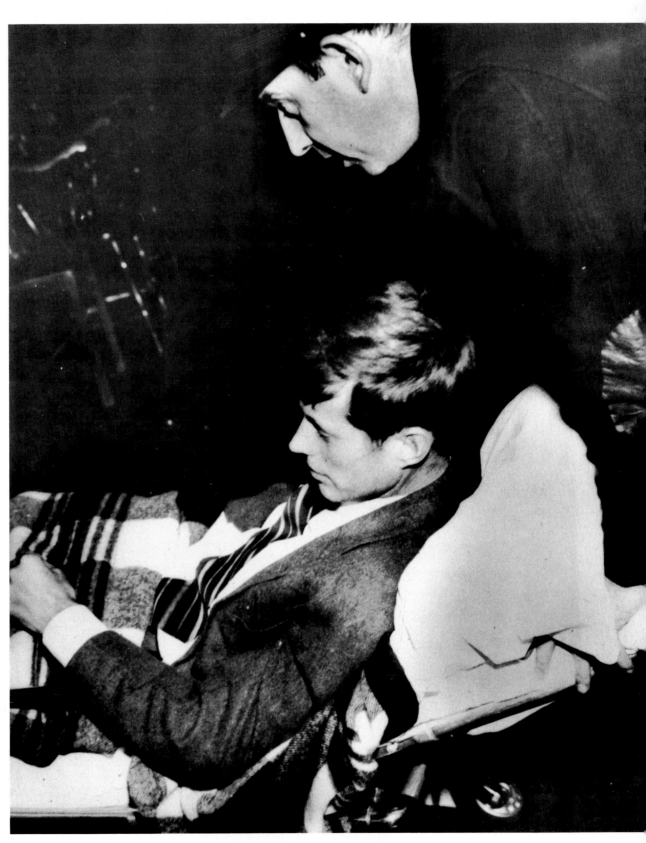

The family kept it quiet that Addison's disease was the cause of Jack's frequent collapses. Here he was entering a Boston hospital to be treated, the Kennedys said, for a recurrence of malaria from his South Pacific days. To add to his general poor health was a chronically painful back. Much too light to be playing football at Harvard, he had ruptured a spinal disk in a scrimmage, an injury that would plague him for the rest of his days.

Chapter 2

STEPPING INTO POLITICS

After breezing to a surprising victory, the young Congressman was photographed by LIFE in Washington with a sheet for a background.

Joseph Kennedy had set his heart on creating the country's first Irish-Catholic President but with Joe Jr.'s death his dream seemed ended. Yet it was not long before his jaunty, fluent second son turned away from journalism and teaching as possible careers and decided for politics. The Ambassador might have his dream after all. "It was like being drafted," Jack recalled. "My father wanted his eldest son in politics. 'Wanted' isn't the right word. He demanded it." Still wearing a brace for his injured back, 29-year-old Jack barnstormed 14 hours a day for the congressional seat representing the 11th Massachusetts District—immigrant territory mostly, with few Yankees to win over. Laughed off at first because of his youth, wealth and lack of experience, the boy who had been a messy and unruly boarder at Choate School a mere decade before now displayed a serious, clean-cut appeal. This, combined with the canny political wisdom of his relatives, the hard work of his siblings and his father's money, made him an easy winner. His course was set, and although he did not distinguish himself in the House, he was ready for his run for the Senate in 1952.

At the 1946 Bunker Hill Day parade in Charlestown, Massachusetts, young Kennedy was about to test his vote-getting talent for the first time.

With hard work and the help of his brother he fought his way into the Senate in 1952

Even though father Joe was pulling the strings and spending the money behind the scenes, Jack's run for a Senate seat in 1952 was a family victory, and it was his campaign manager Robert who stood and read the early returns.

At first Joe Kennedy had little confidence in Jack as a politician; Jack was too shy and lacked the dynamic appeal that had so delighted him in his first son. But one day in East Boston Joe had watched Jack shaking hands with longshoremen. "I would have given odds of 5,000 to 1 that this thing . . . could never have happened," the Ambassador remembered. "I never thought Jack had it in him."

Wooing and winning the votes

In 1952 Joseph Kennedy was all for Jack taking on the incumbent Massachusetts Senator Henry Cabot Lodge II. "When you've beaten Lodge," he said. "you've beaten the best. Why try for something less?" Busy managing General Eisenhower's campaign for President, Lodge arrived home late for his own race. Jack was already using his boyish appeal, his genuine warmth and his quick wit to charm the lady voters at living room teas like this.

Formal receptions made royalty of the Kennedys

Grim-faced, Senator Henry
Cabot Lodge watched
the returns and waited until
7:20 a.m. to concede.

Often Rose was as big a
draw as her son at the
33 formal receptions the
Kennedys held at the
fanciest hotels in the state.
Here Jack beguiled a few
of the tens of thousands
of voters who swarmed to the
carefully planned and
beautifully executed
campaign parties that
helped defeat Lodge.

Chapter 3

*"I leaned across the asparagus
and asked her for a date."*

ENTER JACKIE

In 1951 at a Washington dinner party given by a matchmaking newspaperman friend, the dashing young Congressman wanted to know if the beautiful young lady sitting near him would like to go out. Born in Southampton, schooled at Miss Porter's in Farmington, Connecticut, a recent graduate of George Washington University after two years at Vassar and one at the Sorbonne in Paris, Jacqueline Bouvier was working as the "inquiring photographer" for the *Washington Times-Herald*. A stunning girl with wide-apart eyes and a wistful smile, Jackie was a breed apart from the host of young lovelies Jack normally squired. Aloof, private, independent, possessing esthetic interests and a barbed wit, Jackie had grown up in a broken family, shuttled from one estate to another. Her pleasures were often solitary—reading, riding, listening to music. Even though she was soon swept into the Kennedy family life, she never really felt at home with these ambitious, competitive people whose Boston Irish political sense seemed rowdy. Still, the courtship took hold and flourished. And then, when she was in England in 1953 photographing the coronation of Queen Elizabeth, her zestful, shrewd, playboy beau, now a junior Senator, proposed by cable.

**This picture of Jack and Jackie sailing
made the cover of LIFE, the first of many.**

On the veranda of the Kennedy summer house in Hyannis Port on Cape Cod, Jackie relaxed between sporting events. These and the following pictures were taken for LIFE in July 1953, just two months before the couple's wedding.

Jackie tried an end run around a Kennedy sister.

Jack let go a long pass to Jacqueline who was struggling to get open. Actually, she didn't participate in the highly competitive Kennedy football antics for very long. "If I get the ball, which way do I run?" she once asked in a huddle. After breaking an ankle, she decided to watch the hostilities from the porch, preferably with her father-in-law, who loved her frank talk and occasional gibes.

With Jack as catcher, Jackie displayed a slightly awkward batting style.

Jackie sized up her new family and some of their royal friends from ambassadorial days.

The original magazine caption for this picture said: "Mussing the Senator, Jackie tousles his hair, his political trademark."

With Jackie trying the tiller, Senator Kennedy and his fiancée took a sail off Cape Cod. According to family custom, Kennedy kids were not allowed to sail until they had been tossed into the open sea (with life jackets) so they would know what it was like to panic and therefore be more prepared for sailing accidents.

Even though no longer the inquiring photographer,
Jackie showed she was still adept with a camera.
At first, Jack's jealous sisters called her the Deb,
and made fun of her babylike voice.

Relaxing more informally than he would with the press in the years ahead, Jack and his future bride talked everything but politics, one of Jackie's least favorite subjects back then.

Borrowing the camera for a moment,
Jackie squeezed off a frame of her
fiancé with LIFE's photographer Hy
Peskin (left) and reporter Clay Felker.
Peskin was a top sports photographer
and Felker, today a well-known editor,
worked in LIFE's Sports department.

Jack showed lithe grace while skipping
pebbles out over the surf. His bad
back made him give up tennis but he
did try to keep up his golf.

This was one of the many pictures made up
as covers for the LIFE editors to choose from.

and so . . . "off into the sunset."

Along with something borrowed (her mother's lace handkerchief) and something blue (a garter), Jackie wore her wedding present from Jack—a diamond bracelet. Here at the beginning of the bridal meal, the couple is about to dive into the first course—fruit cup served in hollowed-out half pineapples.

Chapter 4

"Give me a beach and a girl and that's about as good as life can get."

A WEDDING ALBUM

A crowd of 3,000 people broke through police lines and nearly crushed the bride," the *New York Times* began its story on the grand Newport wedding. "The ceremony far surpassed the Astor-French wedding of 1943 . . ." Orchestrated as it was by Joe Kennedy, that was no surprise.

The proceedings began with a five-day house party at Hyannis Port at which 10 bridal attendants and 14 ushers joined the bride and groom in everything from scavenger hunts and sailing races to touch football and charades. The warm-up continued at the bridal dinner, held at Newport's swank Clambake Club, where the country's abdicating "most eligible bachelor" presented each usher with a Brooks Brothers umbrella and the bridal attendants got initialed silver picture frames.

Next morning in Newport's oldest Catholic church the Most Reverend Richard J. Cushing, Archbishop of Boston, read a special blessing from the Pope and celebrated the nuptial mass with communion. Another Boston import, tenor Luigi Vena, sang *Ave Maria.* The bride wore an ivory taffeta dress made of 50 yards of material. Draped from a circle of orange blossoms, her grandmother's wedding veil of rose point lace extended in a flowing train. Jacqueline carried a bouquet of pink and white spray orchids, stephanotis and miniature gardenias. Nowhere to be seen was the bride's father, "Black Jack" Bouvier, who, the gossip went, was too drunk to take his daughter up the aisle. Her stepfather, Hugh D. Auchincloss, filled in.

After the ceremony the ordeal of the reception line ran on for two hours at Auchincloss' 300-acre estate overlooking Narragansett Bay. Guests ranged from Vanderbilt neighbors to House Speaker Joe Martin to movie queen Marion Davies. Played bouncily by society bandmaster Meyer Davis, *I Married an Angel* had been handpicked by the groom for the first dance. Guests feasted on creamed chicken, ice cream in the shape of roses and 35 cases of champagne. The cake came from a baker in Quincy, Massachusetts. Upstairs, several thousand wedding presents were on display, with two truckloads still unopened.

Cake cut, toasts made, dances danced and pictures posed for, Jackie stood at the top of the stairs reciting "eeny, meeny, miny, mo" before tossing down her bouquet, which was caught by bridesmaid Nancy Tuckerman. Then the newlyweds were off to Acapulco.

At the Church...

At the church door the dressmaker holds the bride's train high so it won't get trampled

The bride arrives for the 11 a.m. ceremony

In the absence of her father, Jackie's stepfather, Hugh D. Auchincloss, does the honors

Joe and Rose beaming after the ceremony

The groom's parents arrive, Rose in a gray-blue lace dress and dark red velvet hat

couple kneels at the altar

Man and wife

The happy ex-bachelor

Holding back some of the 2,000 curious

ving church

Reception Line...

Guests line up outside the Auchincloss mansion

The reception line includes not only the bride and groom, Rose Kennedy and the Auchinclosses, but all 10 bridesmaids as well

The Ambassador, followed by Claiborne Pell, maneuvers through the line

The bride takes a break

Jackie peeks out the staircase window at the guests

While the groom taps his teeth, the bride's sister Lee whispers to flower girl Janet Auchincloss, their half-sister

A quiet moment for the groom and the flower girl

After two hours of handshakes and hugs, the bride and groom make their entrance onto the tented outdoor dance floor

Three Kennedys in a row—Bobby, Pat and Papa Joe

The Dance...

Now the bride's stepfather takes his turn

Teddy K. struts with his new sister-in-law

A foxtrot for Bobby

Jack chose *I Married an Angel* for the first dance

The Ambassador cuts in and pumps his left hand high

obby is bug-eyed over the whole ffair

A good view of Granny's veil

Orchids and gardenias rest on Joe's shoulder

tep-brother Hugh Auchincloss Jr. as a cheek-to-cheek

A private sniff

55

Narragansett Bay is the backdrop

Kennedy siblings Bobby, Pat, Eunice, Teddy and Jean gather to serenade their brother and his bride

With her white gloves finally removed, guests could admire the bride's emerald and diamond engagement ring, here hidden by the cake

After the serenade . . . mirth!

The bride respectfully rises when the Ambassador pays her a visit

The groom helps out when the bride cuts the cake

The Feast...

the bridal party only, a special sit-
wn luncheon

Jackie chatters with sister Lee while
Jack communes with fellow Senator and
fun lover George Smathers

A baker in Quincy, Massachusetts
thought up this five-decker

Lee helps with her sister's veil as the
feast breaks up and the wedding party
moves out into the field for pictures

Formal Pictures...

After the feast, the bride, making sure her train follows without catching on the grass, moves slowly to the field that has been selected for the formal pictures, but the high-spirited ushers take every opportunity to display their considerable athletic skills. Once corralled, the men group around the bridegroom for the opening portraits, until Jackie is summoned. Finally, the ladies in waiting are allowed in. In the bottom right-hand picture, starting at left with the back row, the wedding party includes Charles Bartlett, Michael Canfield, George Smathers, Lem Billings, Torbert MacDonald and Charles Spalding. To the right of the bride and groom stand James Reed, Ben Smith, Joseph Gargan, Sargent Shriver, Paul Fay, Teddy Kennedy, Hugh Auchincloss II and Bobby Kennedy. Starting at left again, bridal attendants are: Nancy Tuckerman, Martha Bartlett (in front of Miss Tuckerman), maid-of-honor Nina Auchincloss, matron-of-honor and the bride's sister Lee Bouvier Canfield, Janet Auchincloss, Ethel Kennedy, Shirley Oakes, Jean Kennedy, Aileen Travers, Sylvia Whitehouse and Helen Spaulding.

Leaving...

Some of the help wait at the top of the stairs to see Jackie throw her bouquet

"Eeny, meeny, miny, mo," she counts out each of her bridesmaids below, and then from the landing Jackie flings the bouquet; bridesmaid Nancy Tuckerman caught it

The present room is open for inspection

Changing to a gray suit for traveling, Jackie rejoins her husband and starts to bid their attendants goodbye

Down the stairs they go, into a petal storm of confetti, a grain storm of rice

The storms subside . . .

and the happy couple is off, first to
w York City, thence to Acapulco

THE TROUBLES AND TRIUMPHS AHEAD

For the young romantic Jacqueline, married life was not easy. Her husband either came home late, exhausted, or was away on political trips. During that first year she had a miscarriage. And increasingly she was being humiliated at parties when Jack would slip off with pretty young girls. To her husband's dismay she began obsessively remodeling rooms in their Georgetown house. Though he was personally worth more than $10 million, Jack began nitpicking about his wife's clothing bills.

To add to this mounting tension, intense pain recurred in Kennedy's back and suddenly he found himself on crutches, virtually a cripple. Down in weight from 180 to 140 pounds, in October of '54 he underwent difficult three-hour surgery—a double fusion of the spinal disks—made even more dangerous by the failure of his immune system because of lifelong Addison's disease. A staph infection followed, Kennedy lapsed into a coma and twice was administered the last rites. Somehow he recovered, but having cheated real death he now made a near-fatal political judgment: he did not vote in the Sen-

ate censure of Joe McCarthy, which he could have done from his hospital bed. Taken by stretcher to his family's home in Palm Beach for Christmas, Kennedy remained in agony until a second operation in February finally brought relief. While recuperating, he worked on a book telling the stories of eight political leaders who had sacrificed their careers for the good of America. *Profiles in Courage* was published a year later in 1955 and became an instant best seller.

Back at work Kennedy demonstrated that his interest encompassed the country as a whole and not just the state he represented. He traveled to learn all he could about NATO and Southeast Asia. Most important, by 1956 he was becoming a television idol. Later, Lyndon Johnson would think back on those days: "It was the goddamnedest thing, here was a young whippersnapper, malaria-ridden and yellah, sickly, sickly ... Now, I will admit that he had a good sense of humor and that he looked awfully good on the goddam television screen ... but his growing hold on the American people was simply a mystery to me."

Chapter 5

A NATIONAL FIGURE

Amid the roar and dazzle of their Chicago convention of August 1956, the Democrats chose standard-bearers to feed to the Eisenhower-happy electorate, but America discovered someone else: John F. Kennedy. On the first night the delegates, and the nation, saw and heard a skillfully prepared campaign movie on the party's history produced by Dore Schary and narrated by Kennedy. The next morning, Massachusetts' young war-hero Senator was a national figure, chosen to introduce Stevenson. Soon he was also what he had hesitated to become: a vice-presidential candidate. Father Joe angrily warned him from his rented vacation villa on the Riviera that if he associated himself with Adlai Stevenson's inevitable loss, his Catholicism would be blamed and he would lose the opportunity to run for President in 1960. But in the process of becoming his own man and not a "dummy" as he once put it, with his father playing "ventriloquist," he went for the nomination hard. With Stevenson's decision to leave the nomination to the delegates, New York and, dramatically, Texas put Kennedy ahead of favorite Estes Kefauver on the second ballot. But on the third, Southern states moved toward Kefauver. Kennedy, realizing that he had peaked, reacted quickly and gracefully. He moved that the Tennesseean be nominated by acclamation, and then was gone, a gallant loser who was clearly a long-term winner.

"Some people have their liberalism 'made' by the time they reach their late 20s. I didn't. I was caught in crosscurrents and eddies. It was only later that I got into the stream of things."

Hoopla on the floor and on the rostrum was frenzied as always and, with burgeoning TV introducing a platform of its own (below, right), even better lighted.

After his film narration, Kennedy, no longer just a voice-over but a leading voice of his party, was buttonholed by the press wherever he moved.

Pregnant Jackie was cool amid the pandemonium

Jacqueline, sharing Jack's reflected glory with his sister Eunice Shriver from the front row of the mezzanine, was in the final months of her second pregnancy, her first having ended in a miscarriage.

Calm, almost bemused, wife of the man of the hour the waves of politi emotion roll over her. But b home soon afterward, w her husband relaxed in a p atmosphere on a yacht in Mediterranean, Jackie 28, lost the second child, a

Frank Sinatra, his liberal credentials and his voice in top shape, got the big show off with a minute of unity, singing the national anthem.

Once he (belatedly) got accreditation to the main floor, Senator Kennedy found himself a cynosure (above) wherever he drifted. His brother Robert (left), an expert buttonholer himself, was his campaign manager even before he had a campaign to manage.

Southern votes for the young newcomer
were largely swipes at Kefauver's
Senate anticrime campaign, but one big one
almost made him the vice-presidential candidate.

A dramatic moment came when, after the New York delegation's vote on the second vice-presidential ballot put Kennedy in a strong position vs. front runner Kefauver, the Texans caucused and showed their hands for Kennedy too (above). A few minutes later back in the auditorium, Lyndon Johnson boomed, "Texas proudly casts its vote for the fighting sailor who wears the scars of battle." Kennedy won the ballot and was only 33½ votes short of victory.

The gallant runner-up cut a figure . . .

Introduced by the chairman, House
Speaker Sam Rayburn, Kennedy moved
to make Kefauver the vice-presidential
candidate by acclamation, giving
Convention watchers nationwide
a preview of gestures and body
language that would one day
be familiar to the whole world.

Unity again prevailed as Harry Truman and his defeated presidential protégé, Averell Harriman, stood with the winning ticket, Adlai Stevenson and Estes Kefauver, before an erupting International Amphitheater.

The best of all possible worlds for Kennedy:
a shining future unthreatened by the
defeat that awaited the week's victors

1
co
sp
ou
Wi
ch
na
lec

wh
pla
for
Ca
be
of

inc
ne
fac
sue

inc
ty's
tior
am
it w
pul
tha
nat
age
tior

mu

so
w

Ma

Spent but happy, Kefauver paused before leaving
the podium with his running mate to grasp the
hand of the man who almost beat him in the
closest vice-presidential battle in party history.

social insurance programs still await many of those who are unemployed, disabled, or "too old to work and too young to die."

▶ An all-time record of over 65 million people are at work, but nearly two thirds of them will continue to have no federal protection against substandard wages unless we can greatly expand the coverage of the Fair Labor Standards Act. Dozens of pockets of chronic unemployment persisting in many states need federal loans and contracts, technical assistance, supplemental jobless benefits and other methods of relief and encouragement.

▶ Businessmen, large and small, concerned about the increasing number of business failures and mergers as money tightens, need old legislation improved to meet these new problems.

▶ Hundreds of thousands of small farmers, foreclosed or merged out of existence as the combined burdens of drought, falling prices and rising costs have proved too much to bear, need new solutions to solve old problems.

▶ The blight, decay and delinquency that plague our aging cities, inequities in taxation, power shortages, fiscal policies, immigration restrictions—these and a host of other problems can be postponed, ignored or swept under the rug, but not for long.

▶ Let it not be said that we are fearful or incapable of solving with fairness and forthrightness the sensitive, complex issue of race relations. The Democratic party is best equipped to provide responsible leadership in this area: first, because we are a national party, including within our membership both a majority of Negroes and a majority of Southerners; and secondly, because we have always, as a party, emphasized human values and human ideals. I, for one, do not share the view that Negro voters are leaving the Democratic party for good. A majority is still with us because it judges the two parties on their records and leadership on a variety of issues rather than on the civil rights statements of a few prominent figures.

5. Democratic spokesmen in and out of Congress must be willing to offer constructive opposition in the field of foreign policy. "Modern Republicanism" has not eliminated all differences between the parties on foreign affairs. Many alarming problems are in need of careful scrutiny. Among them are: the validity and responsibility of Mr. Dulles' policy statements and administration, the authority of the executive and legislative branches, our policies in the Middle East and Asia, our relations with our Western allies, our neglect of the good neighbor policy carefully nurtured by Cordell Hull, our answer to the challenge of nationalism and colonialism, the questions of disarmament and atomic control, the deterioration of our comparative defense strength. The party in control of the executive branch cannot reasonably be expected to offer self-examination and criticism (we Democrats didn't when we were in). Thus only the opposition party offers a channel for legitimate concern and dissent on foreign policy—dissent without disunity. But our own uncertainties and divisions over such basic issues as trade, economic aid and executive prerogatives—recently demonstrated by our votes on the Mideast doctrine—must to the extent possible be replaced by a positive consensus that gives the nation a clear alternative.

6. Finally, and perhaps most important of all, Democrats on the local level must be willing to substi-

When Teddy, the baby of the family, married in November 1958, the nuptial dinner served not only to welcome the former Joan Bennett to the family but also to celebrate the overwhelming re-election to the Senate of the best man, J.F.K. Jack shared the occasion's warm glow with his kid brother the bridegroom behind the veiled head of the day's leading lady.

A brother team, Senator John and committee counsel Robert, put their heads together at a 1957 hearing of a Senate select committee on labor racketeering.

tute new life and new leadership for the luxury of petty local factionalism. With a new breed of respected, dynamic professional politicians coming into prominence, we can no longer afford to continue in official party positions tired or tarnished holdovers from another era—men whose stature and activities inspire neither the enthusiasm of volunteer workers nor the respect of their communities—men who keep busy by attending meetings, filing gloomy forecasts and complaints, and fighting zealously to hold on to their positions.

We need another kind of local worker and leader in our party, men and women such as those I met last fall in all regions and particularly in the West—full of enthusiasm, full of new ideas, full of determination, asking nothing in return. Not many of them could buy tickets to the $100-a-plate dinners where few votes are changed, but they could all ring doorbells or hold neighborhood teas. Most of them were the younger members of our party, others were at least young in spirit. But all possessed vigor our party can use all over the country. The future of our party hinges upon this kind of new life and leadership, from the precinct level on up to the host of newly prominent young Democratic governors and senators: Muskie of Maine, Ribicoff of Connecticut, Gore and Clement of Tennessee, Meyner of New Jersey, Williams of Michigan, Clark and Leader of Pennsylvania, Collins and Smathers of Florida, Neuberger of Oregon, Johnson of Texas, Mansfield of Montana, Humphrey of Minnesota, Symington of Missouri, Jackson of Washington and a whole host elected in 1956, as well as other leaders who have long served the nation as governors, mayors or in the Congress.

I have offered no single magic formula for a successful Democratic party and I have proposed no candidates for a winning ticket for 1960. For their identity, I believe, is less important than their capacity for wise, progressive, responsible leadership; their methods of campaigning for victory are less significant than the principles that guide their party.

For "the success of a party means little," as Woodrow Wilson said in his first Inaugural, "except when the Nation is using that party for a large and definite purpose." The task of the Democratic party during the next four years is to define such a purpose for all the nation; and success, I have no doubt, will then be rightfully ours in 1960 and the years beyond.

Chapter 6

THE MAKING OF A KING AND QUEEN

Once upon a time . . . From the moment of his lucky near-miss at Chicago, John Kennedy's story started to read less like a Washington novel and more like the kind of tale that starts with that age-old phrase. Before the next year was out, Jacqueline gave birth to a healthy and beautiful baby, Caroline. Even before she arrived, the Senator set off in pursuit of the dream whose time, even his father now agreed, had come. He wrote many more articles for national publications and got on many more magazine covers. By the time he announced his candidacy in 1960, he had talked to the citizens and pumped the hands of Democratic leaders in all 50 states, accompanied on his travels by Theodore C. Sorensen, a speechwriter 11 years his junior with a wit to match his own and an ear for his New England cadences. He had also given unprecedented access to a few chosen photographers, who produced irresistible picture stories of what was clearly the ideal American family.

"Nobody is going to hand me the nomination. When the time is ripe, I'll have to work for it. If I were governor of a large state, Protestant and fifty-five, I could sit back and let it come to me."

An intimate portrait of Jackie, part of a LIFE essay on her "cultured, quiet, unpolitical" life at home in Georgetown while "front runner" Jack was in and out campaigning, was one of the fruits of the couple's association with photographer Mark Shaw.

Picture-book parents and a baby born for the lens

If Nina Leen captured the essence
of mother love, it was Ed Clark
who caught Caroline (at four months!)
as the quintessential flirt,
in a classic baby picture.

A couple of fellows watching Caroline's eyes

The peekaboo shot was one of a series Clark took while J.F.K. and he followed the baby's bobbing head and roving gaze—which always of course returned to Daddy.

The fatherly pride that Kennedy's lifelong friend Kirk (Lem) Billings noted in him showed clearly in this Clark portrait. "Jack was more emotional about Caroline's birth than he was about anything else," Billings told biographer Doris Kearns Goodwin.

When Jackie, as she loved to do, walked in tranquillity along Washington's Chesapeake & Ohio Canal, Shaw was part of the landscape.

A weekend away from politics

Flying in from Washington, Jack was greeted with a long-time-no-see hug from Jackie.

Checking out the clan kids, J.F.K. found Jackie and Caroline watching, somewhat warily, a pride of small Kennedys playing under a porch shower, one, at the pull-chain, daring the others to dash through when he turned it off.

Horsing around

At her mother's place in Virginia, Jackie could indulge in her favorite physical exercise, with a companion guaranteed not to talk politics.

Relaxation came most easily to J.F.K. at family retreats. At Hyannis Port it was like taking candy from a baby (Caroline was in a generous mood this day). And tossing her skyward (below) was one sport that never hurt his injured back.

Chapter 7

GOING FOR IT!

"I suppose anybody in politics would like to be President . . . that is the center of action, the mainspring, the wellspring of the American system."

When, on Jan. 20, 1960, Senator Kennedy announced his candidacy, he knew that his political glad-handing of the past three years, for all the ties it had established with leaders and future convention delegates, was not enough. Many of the big delegations were still controlled by powerful bosses, who were not convinced he could reach the ordinary voter, and the only way to show them he could was to win presidential primaries in key states. The second of the seven he chose, Wisconsin's wild, open (with party machinery forbidden) April vote, was the most formidable. He would be opposed by Hubert Humphrey, a vote getter from next door Minnesota. Starting in the March snows, J.F.K. and his siblings, headed by Robert, his campaign manager, crisscrossed the state. Jack demonstrated his command of the issues in both farming (largely Protestant) and industrial (heavily Catholic) counties. The rest of the clan was loosing the Kennedy charm and energy on Badgers in every walk of life. On election eve political prognosticators called it a walkover for Kennedy. It was far from that. He won, but his margin was soberingly slender. Humphrey took it as a moral victory. And the really bad news was that the voters had split along religious lines. It meant, as Jack told one of his sisters, that "we have to do it all over again," to win every primary ahead, "West Virginia and Maryland and Indiana and Oregon, all the way to the convention" in Los Angeles.

"I am announcing today my candidacy for the presidency of the United States," the Senator from Massachusetts confidently told the Washington press corps in the Senate Caucus Room.

Even before his announcement, Kennedy had started his Wisconsin campaign, addressing the state Democratic convention in Milwaukee in November 1959.

Formidable Wisconsin

Softening up Wisconsin the previous November for the March primary blitz, J.F.K. had maintained a schedule that had him holding strategy meetings on trains, slurping soup at station counters and addressing luncheon audiences who had awaited his delayed arrival.

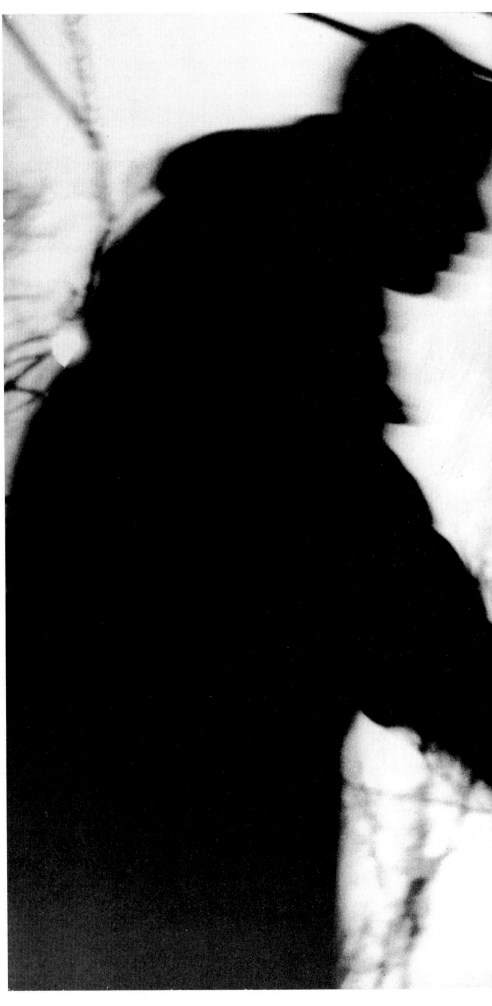

"Ted Kennedy—John's brother," said the youngest
of the candidate's family task force for the
Wisconsin primary, handshaking at dawn at the
gate of the Oscar Meyer plant in Madison.

The Kennedy siblings turned out in force

LIFE's cover story on t[...]
campaign followed bo[...]
candidates all over t[...]
state. It also followed J.F.K[...]
bush-beating sibling[...]
which burned [...]
great amounts of film. (T[...]
photograph at rig[...]
originally appeared on LIF[...]
cover, as did a number [...]
others in this boo[...]

Visiting the Menominee reservation in Keshena, the candidate signed autographs (on whatever surface was convenient and comfortable) and Jackie danced with the menfolk.

Sister Pat, who as actor Peter Lawford's wife lent Hollywood glamour to the Kennedy troops, handed out postcard requests for literature (right) at a Madison kaffeeklatsch. Below, the three sisters, Eunice Shriver, Jean Smith and Pat, regrouped in front of the state capitol and Teddy re-enlisted as a gladhander.

His sweep in the Mountain State removed his greatest rival and sent him really on his way

Kennedy, so sure of victory this time that he had returned to Washington to hear the returns in private, flew to Charleston in the wee hours and, in the Kanawha Hotel, gripped Humphrey's hand, as did Jacqueline (below). "It was very nice of you to come over, Hubert," he told the tearful loser.

After he read the *Washington Post's* story of his victory the following dawn, a newsman asked Kennedy, "What are you going to do now?" His reply: "I have to study up on the problems of Maryland tonight. I'm campaigning there tomorrow."

Chapter 8

NOMINATION

"I tell you the New Frontier is here, whether we seek it or not. Beyond that frontier are unchartered areas of science and space, unsolved problems of peace and war, unconquered pockets of ignorance and prejudice, and unanswered questions of poverty and surplus . . . I am asking you to be new pioneers on that New Frontier."

The road to triumphant pandemonium in the Los Angeles Memorial Sports Arena and Coliseum pictured below started the moment Kennedy returned to Hyannis Port from his character-building 1956 defeat. As a devil's advocate, he ticked off for his father all the reasons he should not run for President in 1960 and after Joe, predictably, shot down each one, Kennedy said, "Well, Dad, when do we start?"

From then on, everything a presidential hopeful could desire came his way. His beautiful wife had a beautiful baby. He won a post on the prestigious Senate Foreign Relations Committee. He received a Pulitzer Prize for his 1956 book, *Profiles in Courage*. In 1958 he won a second term by a whopping 73.6 percent. When he hit the campaign trail, he won all seven of his target primaries, losing none.

Despite his unshakable confidence, he deployed, at the Convention as on the road, the most efficient campaign organization ever fielded by a candidate. (He had operatives with virtually every state delegation, eight of them carrying walkie-talkies with which he could communicate individually or all at once.)

He had a qualm or two (Johnson was said to be bad-mouthing him, Stevenson won a heart-stirring ovation, and Eleanor Roosevelt called him "too much profile, not enough courage"), but he never seriously doubted he would win—"because," as President Roosevelt had once said in a different context, "we planned it that way."

The arena rang with words and music

Actor Tony Curtis and singer Frank Sinatra were a little island of show-biz amid the politicos. Sinatra had done plenty of politicking for Jack, having turned his hit movie tune *High Hopes* into a campaign song that he sang countless times along the primary trail.

Brother Bobby worked the floor with unflagging energy, applying his campaign-manager principle that man's reach should exceed his grasp.

The candidate and two powerhouses of the family team, sister Pat Lawford, here on her home turf, and mother Rose, joined voices in the national anthem.

Confident Kennedy addressed his own Massachusetts delegation. The morning of the day balloting was to start he spoke before six state caucuses.

A great little debate at a crucial juncture

Against the advice of his brain trust, Kennedy accepted presidential hopeful Lyndon Johnson's challenge to a debate before his own Texas delegation. The Senate Majority Leader (top right), his words carried to the entire convention by closed-circuit TV, made sport of "young Jack," his "innocence" and his "inexperience," and alluded to the Senate absenteeism of "some people." Although L.B.J., joined by Lady Bird and daughter Lynda (right), got a good hand, J.F.K.'s graceful response ("I assume he was talking about some other candidate, not me," he said of his Senate record) just about ended the Johnson bid.

One-two punch of power and charm

J.F.K. and R.F.K. put their heads together, planning grand strategy, in Suite 8315 on the eighth floor of Los Angeles' Hotel Biltmore, where the Chief received bulletins from his private tabulating center five floors below.

After the debate, smiling Bobby followed up his brother's disarming of Johnson. "I come here today," J.F.K. had told the Texans, "full of admiration for Senator Johnson, full of affection for him, strongly in support of him—for majority leader."

The first casualty of a run for the White House is privacy

After a day taken up with a post-nomination press conference and a swim, J.F.K. flew to Hyannis Port Sunday night to find the house (left and below) ablaze with television lights. The high-profile stage of his quest had arrived.

A rainy day dampened camera crews and pushed reporters into the intimacy of a porch press conference. But the sun did shine on Daddy's efforts to take a break with Caroline and her mom (below).

The not-so-private enclave at Hyannis Port

House guests who had come a long way were Jack's running mate, L.B.J., and Lady Bird, who posed with their hosts.

Chapter 9

ALL OUT FOR ELECTION

When, at 8:30 p.m. Chicago time, on Sept. 26, some 70 million Americans tuned in to the highly publicized confrontation between John Kennedy and Richard Nixon in the first of four scheduled debates, they knew they were watching history. But few were aware that they were seeing the first presidential election ever to be *shaped* by television. TV's largest audience ever had been the 90 million who saw the Los Angeles Dodgers beat the Chicago White Sox in six games in the 1959 World Series, and more than that probably saw at least one of the debates. The beneficiary of this concentration was Kennedy. Once again, fortune smiled upon him—helped along, of course, by his poise and preparation. The camera was as kind to his light Celtic skin and gently rounded features as it was harsh to the haggard Nixon. Kennedy came across as patrician, relaxed, in command of facts and issues. Nixon appeared tense, nearly ill, and he sweated through the powder he had applied against "5-o'clock shadow." Going into the debate, Nixon was a slight favorite; when it was over J.F.K. had clearly gained ground. Radio listeners polled the next day thought the opponents were about even; TV watchers gave it all to Jack. From then on, wherever he went on the campaign trail—and he covered 44,000 miles between Labor Day and Election Day—he was greeted by wildly cheering crowds.

On camera in CBS's Chicago studio (CBS staged the first debate for all three networks, bumping *The Andy Griffith Show* in the process), Nixon was gaunt with campaign fatigue; Kennedy looked starting-line fresh. J.F.K. made his points graciously; Nixon frequently glowered. And while Nixon directed his thrusts and parries at his opponent, Kennedy addressed the audience.

*"Every time I get in the middle of a day
I look down at the schedule and there's five minutes
allotted for the candidate to eat and rest."*

"We must climb to the hilltop"

Making his grueling traversals of the country to take his debate-constricted message directly to the voters, Kennedy was required to formulate his political philosophy. This need happily coincided with the desires of LIFE. Editor-in-chief Henry R. Luce had raised a question about whether the U.S. was a people who had arrived and now had no place to go. He had charged LIFE and its sister magazines to explore "The National Purpose." LIFE asked J.F.K., among others, to address this issue, and the eloquent essay with which he responded embraced all the things he was saying on the hustings. It follows in its entirety.

In all recorded history, probably the sagest bit of advice ever offered man was the ancient admonition to "know thyself." As with individuals, so with nations. Just as a man who realizes that his life has gone off course can regain his bearings only through the strictest self-scrutiny, so a whole people, become aware that things have somehow gone wrong, can right matters only by a rigidly honest look at its core of collective being, its national purpose.

Thus, while on the one hand the fact that we have felt the urge to debate our national purpose signalizes our arrival at a potential crisis point, on the other hand the fact that we have entered into the debate willingly, indeed with gusto, bodes well for the eventual outcome.

Among our overindulgences of the past decade has been the lavish use of a kind of cloudy rhetoric that only befogs the truth. Yet basically we Americans prefer plain talk and common sense. It is these we must apply if we are to "know ourselves" again.

(continued)

Kennedy volunteers, in familiar high-key attire, were squeezed tightly up front when their candidate addressed a monster crowd.

The facets of this debate on national purpose are many. Other than to agree that the whole subject vitally needs airing, the debaters are split a dozen ways as to which aspect of it demands greatest emphasis. Some prefer to dwell on what has happened to our national purpose—whether irrevocably lost, permanently strayed or temporarily sidetracked; others on why what has happened has happened; others on what can be done by way of remedy or reprieve. Above all, the debate turns on precisely what this "purpose" is that, momentarily or forever, has gone from our midst.

The distinguished contributors to previous instalments of this LIFE series have offered a variety of definitions of our national purpose, all of them valid. From this it can be seen that no one word or catch phrase will suffice to pinpoint it. Our national purpose is resident, obviously, in the magnificent principles of the Declaration of Independence and of the Constitution and Bill of Rights. It also plainly appears in the writings of Jefferson, Madison and Hamilton, in the words of Jackson and Lincoln, in the works of Emerson and Whitman, in the opinions of Marshall and Holmes, in Wilson's New Freedom and Franklin D. Roosevelt's Four Freedoms. In

As his autocade progressed down the Grand Concourse in the Bronx in New York City, a bride entering a hotel for her wedding reception hailed Kennedy. The candidate spotted her (far left), leaped from his car and made her day with the two-handed handclasp (above) that was his warmest greeting short of the kiss he reserved for babies and old ladies.

common, all of these pulse with a sense of idealistic aspiration, of the struggle for a more perfect Union, of the effort to build the good society as well as the good life here and in the rest of the world.

There is, I think, still another way to describe our national purpose. This definition, while almost a literal one, is nevertheless not a narrow one. It is that our national purpose consists of the combined purposefulness of each of us *when we are at our moral best:* striving, risking, choosing, making decisions, engaging in a pursuit of happiness that is strenuous, heroic, exciting and exalted. When we do so as individuals, we make a nation that, in Jefferson's words, will always be "in the full tide of successful experiment."

(continued)

Such a definition, because it implies a constant, restless, confident questing, neither precludes nor outmodes, but rather complements, the expression of national purpose set forth in our Declaration, our Constitution, and in the words of our great Presidents, jurists and writers. The purpose they envisioned can, indeed, never be outmoded because it has never been and can never be fully achieved. It will always be somewhere just out of reach, a challenge to further aspiring, struggling, striving and searching. Quest has always been the dominant note of our history, whether a quest for national independence; a quest for personal liberty and economic opportunity on a new continent from which the rest of mankind could take heart and hope; a quest for more land, more knowledge, more dignity; a quest for more effective democracy; a quest for a world of free and pacific nations.

It should be said at once that no nation has a corner on striving and aspiring any more than on virtue and compassion. Thus our national purpose finds echo in the minds of men of good intent everywhere. But our purpose may differ from others in the particular background against which it evolved, and by three fundamental facts about us:

First, Americans, more than other peoples, have since independence cherished a strong sense of destiny.

Second, we have always been optimists about our national future. Down through the decades we have had our indentured servants, our slaves and Simon Legrees, our sweated immigrants, our Okies, our depressed and discouraged folk of many stripes. But we have been

(continued)

Kennedy was often met with a blizzard of confetti. In some places the precipitation was so intense that when the doors of his convertible were opened the stuff poured out like water from a tank.

unfailingly confident of winning through all obstacles to realize our dream.

Third, Americans have always been willing to experiment. With no feudal inheritance, with little dead weight of caste or tradition, we have ever been in the mood for bold adventure. Our forefathers would not have tossed aside old associations and crossed the seas without it. New frontiers have always seemed unfolding on our horizon.

With these basic considerations, and because of them, the pace of change in this land has been faster than anywhere else on the globe. The change has been far less noisy and melodramatic than in Russia or China, among others, for since 1865 it has lacked any real elements of violence. We believe in progress by evolution, not revolution. But for precisely this reason the progress has been deeper, saner and more continuously rapid. In our energy, our resourcefulness and our powers of organization, we can assert that the United States has been and is the most dynamic nation in history.

Since this is so, why then our current widespread sense of staleness, of frustration; why the gnawing feeling that we may have lost our way? In my mind there are two broad answers.

One is that the very abundance which our dynamism has created has weaned and wooed us from the tough condition in which, heretofore, we have approached whatever it is we have had to do. A man with extra fat will look doubtfully on attempting

(continued)

On a swing through northern California, J.F.K. reached the scene of an Oakland rally after dark, to be greeted nonetheless by the usual— and gratifying—sea of hands.

The hands and faces of America pressed in on Kennedy as he stumped the nation, particularly those of the women. Democratic Senator Paul Douglas (Illinois) publicly classified J.F.K.'s female followers as "jumpers, shriekers, huggers, lopers and touchers." LIFE illustrated Douglas' taxonomy and added some categories of its own, including gaspers, gogglers, swooners and collapsers. In just one swing, photographer Paul Schutzer captured the specimens on these pages and many more.

the four-minute mile; a nation replete with goods and services, confident that "there's more where that came from," may feel less ardor for questing.

The second answer is that we have, of late, lacked the leadership we require—human frailty being what it is—to remind us of our national purpose, to direct its shaping for current ends, to spur us to new efforts, to encourage and, if need be, to exhort.

In his stirring speech at Queen's Hall in London seeking World War I volunteers, David Lloyd George, soon to be Britain's Prime Minister, described a snug valley in his native Wales. Nestled between the mountains and the sea, shielded from the storms and stresses of the outside world, that little valley offered its inhabitants a placid and sheltered life. But on occasion, Lloyd George recalled, the young men of the valley would refuse to stay put. They would climb its highest hill to be inspired by the majestic peaks in the distance, to have their energies sharpened by the mountain breezes.

Too many Americans in the 1950s, I believe, have been living too much of the time in such a valley. We have felt contented and complacent and comfortable. Now it is time once again to climb to the hilltop, to be reinvigorated and reinspired by those faraway peaks, the principles that are vital to our national greatness, that underlie our national purpose, that foster our "American dream."

Whether we see them or not, those peaks never change. Whether we remember it or not, their meaning never diminishes.

Thus the task that lies ahead is not to create a new national purpose, but to try to recapture the old one. This is no call to retrogression, for this purpose, born

(continued)

184 years ago, will be as noble and as fresh 184 years hence—and beyond.

It it those same old slogans and same old solutions, surrounding the national purpose, that we must guard against. The old ways will not do. They cannot do. The Census Bureau predicts that, if the present curve of growth continues, our population will reach 260 million in only 20 years. When we think of how this increase alone will clothe all our problems in growing urgency, we know that when we once again seize hold of our purpose, we will have to do so with new ideas and new vigor.

Where and how do we apply our national purpose to the challenges of 1960?

Survival is often listed as the major challenge today, and certainly other issues are overshadowed by the one issue that could render the rest moot. But although our physical safety as a nation is more imperiled than ever before in our history, survival

Despite her doctor's warning, pregnant Jackie joined J.F.K. stumping New York City. Garment-center crowds covered 12 blocks.

alone is insufficient as an expression of national purpose. Mere physical survival, at the cost of our way of life, would be worth little; more importantly, survival alone is hardly an aspiration worthy of a great nation. The nobleman who, when asked what he did in the French Revolution, replied, "I survived," may have been hailed for his wit but for little else.

We remember too seldom that survival is threatened not only by ever more awesome weapons of death and destruction but also by a lack of aim and aspiration. Outside the walls of every nation that has grown fat and overly fond of itself has always lurked a lean and hungry enemy.

Competition with that enemy is today deemed by some to be our major challenge; but it, too, reflects our national purpose inadequately. We are, indeed, in competition with the Soviets, and to a large extent our hopes for the future rest on our comparative efforts in economic growth, in the arms race, in scientific achieve-

"If he lost," she said, "I'd never forgive myself for not being there to help." A motorcycle cop called the crush worse than Omaha Beach.

ment, in aid to other nations, in propaganda, in prestige and in a host of other fields.

But we will err tragically if we make competition with the Communists an end in itself. Whatever we do in the name of that competition—improving our race relations, expanding our economy, helping new nations, exploring outer space and all the rest—we ought to be doing anyway, for its own sake, whether competition exists or not.

Peace is humanity's deepest longing, and with the failure to achieve it all other aspirations fail too. In acclaiming it as the major expression of our national purpose, however, we must know what sort of peace we mean. Certainly the unjust peace of subjugation, the uneasy peace of cold war or the fruitless peace of an interval between hot wars is far from a goal that will satisfy.

Prosperity, like peace, is desired by all, and our political orators have traditionally held out the goal of personal and national economic well-being as a primary American aim. But the good life falls short as an indicator of national purpose unless it goes hand in hand with the good society. Even in material terms, prosperity is not enough when there is no equal opportunity to share in it; when economic progress means overcrowded cities, abandoned farms, technological unemployment, polluted air and water, and littered parks and countrysides; when those too young to earn are denied their chance to learn; when those no longer earning live out their lives in lonely degradation.

No single one of these four challenges—survival, competition, peace, prosperity—sums up our national purpose today. The creation of a more perfect Union requires the

pursuit of a whole series of ideals, ideals which can never be fully attained, but the eternal quest for which embodies the American National Purpose:

The fulfillment of every individual's dignity and potential.

The perfection of the democratic process.

The education of every individual to his capacity.

The elimination of ignorance, prejudice, hate and the squalor in which crime is bred.

The elimination of slums, poverty and hunger.

Protection against the economic catastrophes of illness, disability and unemployment.

The achievement of a constantly expanding economy, without inflation or dislocation, ei-

Kennedy's motorcade passed in review before women who waved and saluted him with ruffles and flourishes on cymbals improvised from garbage-can lids.

ther in the factory or on the farm.

The conquest of dread diseases.

The enrichment of American culture.

The attainment of world peace and disarmament, based on world law and order, on the mutual respect of free peoples and on a world economy in which there are no "have-not" or "under-developed" nations.

A dream? Of course—the American dream. No candidate for office, unless he were foolish or deceitful, would *promise* its fulfillment. But we are in urgent need of public men who will *work* toward its fulfillment, guiding, directing and encouraging the popular impetus toward that end.

That this impetus exists is beyond question. We are not a people in panic or despair. We have not "gone over the hill" of history. We have simply, and fortuitously, begun to recognize that somehow we have gotten off the track, and that to get back on we will need stern effort, spirited leadership and common sacrifice.

(continued)

If we are to recharge our sense of national purpose, we should accept no invitations to relax on a patent mattress stuffed with woolly illusions labeled peace, prosperity and normalcy. We should congratulate ourselves not for our country's past glories and present accumulations but for our opportunities for further toil and risk. Rather than take satisfaction in goals already reached, we should be contrite about the goals unreached. We ought not to look for excuses in the budget, but for justifications in the dizzying rush of events and in the harsh realities of our time.

For these are harsh times. The future will not be easier. Our responsibilities will not lessen. Our enemies will not weaken. We must demonstrate that we can meet our responsibility as a free society—that we can by voluntary means match their ruthless exploitation of human, natural and material resources—that freedom can not only compete and survive but prevail and flourish.

It is not enough to debate "What is the meaning of America?" Each of us must also decide "What does it mean to be an American?" Upon us destiny has lavished special favors of liberty and opportunity—and it therefore has demanded of us special efforts, particularly in times such as these.

It requires each one of us to be a little more decent, alert, intelligent, compassionate and resolute in our daily lives—that we exercise our civic duties, whether paying taxes or electing Presidents, with extra pride and care—that we use our freedom of choice to pursue our own destiny in a manner that advances the national destiny, in the work we produce, the subjects we study, the positions we seek, the languages we learn, the complaints we voice, the leaders we follow, the inconveniences we endure.

(continued)

Besides picturing Americans as the peripatetic Kennedy saw them on the campaign circuit, Schutzer pictured the candidate as those Americans did *not* see him—off the hustings. On planes and trains between appearances, J.F.K. found snatches of time and space in which to hobnob with reporters, reflect on what he had seen, tune out the roar of combat and—what else?—polish his next speech.

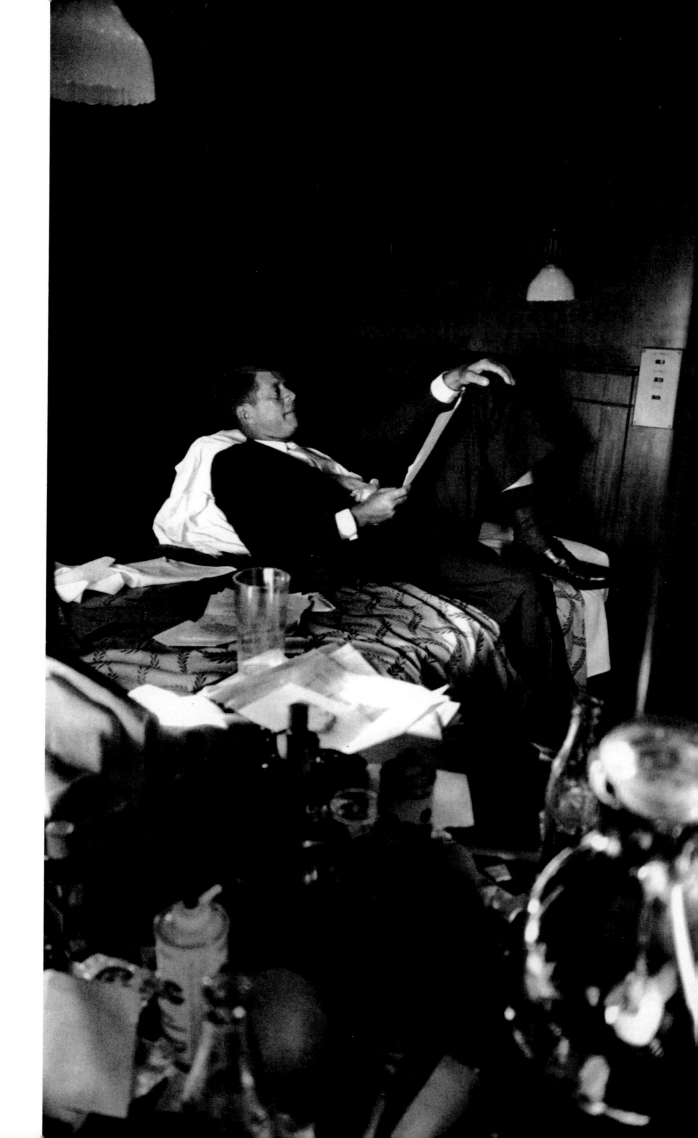

If a dark corner of Africa needs technicians—if a troubled spot in Asia needs language specialists—if a Soviet threat in Berlin requires patience and determination—if the space race requires better schools—we must and can demonstrate that the dedicated efforts of free men can meet these needs better than the efforts of totalitarian compulsion.

Every American must take far more seriously than he has in the past decade his responsibility for achieving and maintaining a democratic society of a truly model kind, worthy to be the champion of freedom throughout the world.

We Americans must again commit ourselves to great ends. We must resume our searching, surging, questing. Then, assuredly, we will come nearer the vision of John Adams of Massachusetts, who, in 1813, assured his friend Thomas Jefferson that our republic would some day "introduce the perfection of man."

Under the incandescent dome of the packed Dallas Memorial Auditorium and the blue sky of Texas, Kennedy punched out, with the right jab that was becoming as familiar as Sugar Ray Robinson's, his message that he would get the U.S. moving again.

149

The Kennedy touch, here mesmerizing a Dallas admirer, became a prize sought by females of all ages. They pushed through crowds, reaching forward to touch and be touched. J.F.K. enjoyed the phenomenon and used it to advantage. But the LIFE team with him reported that when it threatened to get out of hand, he seemed suddenly abashed.

On election night in Hyannis Port the tension was almost palpable

The Kennedy family and friends (including LIFE's Paul Schutzer, who took this picture) clustered at the foot of the stairs in Robert Kennedy's house and listened to returns that poured in from TV, radio and news tickers manned by Bobby and his staff. From left: Rose Kennedy, adviser Ted Sorensen, Sargent Shriver, Jack's prep-school classmate Lem Billings, Jean Smith, Stephen Smith and Peter Lawford.

The morning after: salt air and the sweet smell of success

Morning found Jacqueline walking the familiar edge of Nantucket Sound, adjusting gradually to the idea that she would really be moving to the White House. Jack had waked her at 4 a.m. to tell her that after a night of doubt it looked all right; before her walk she had learned that California had made victory definite.

After the long battle, triumph—and tears

Three years short of a century after "Honey Fitz" Fitzgerald's birth in a North Boston tenement, his descendants were his country's First Family, smiling in triumph in the Hyannis Port home of the President-elect's parents. From left: Ethel Kennedy, Stephen Smith, Eunice Shriver, Jean Smith, Rose and Joseph P. Kennedy, J.F.K., Robert Kennedy, Jackie (looking back at her husband), Pat Lawford, Sargent Shriver (behind seated Ted), Joan Kennedy and Peter Lawford. This was the first time since before the convention that Joseph Kennedy had appeared with his son in public.

At the Ambassador Hotel in Los Angeles, the saddened Nixons appeared before Republican workers as the last California returns indicated their cause was lost. Pat's eyes were tear-filled. Though Nixon acknowledged Kennedy would win "if the present trend continues," he never did concede defeat. When Kennedy's aides, watching him on TV, took caustic note of that, J.F.K. said curtly, "Why should he concede? I wouldn't."

Chapter 10

CORONATION

"And so, my fellow Americans: ask not what your country can do for you— ask what you can do for your country."

The first flakes fell around noon on Inauguration eve, and by nighttime the White House was a winter palace. It was clear that Washington would have what no one had been dreaming of—a white In-

augural. When the First Lady-to-be and her escort left for the star-studded pre-Inaugural gala (below), they stepped gingerly along a path cleared through an eight-inch snowfall. It was a far cry from Camelot, where *The snow may never slush upon the hillside/ By nine p.m. the moonlight must appear.* Though the huge fund raiser began two hours behind schedule, most of the $100-a-head guests did mush their way to the National Guard armory, some of them in VIP buses flowing with champagne and music. Jackie and J.F.K. even got to the Inaugural concert, which started with only 40 members of the National Symphony in their chairs.

The stars came out anyway

Almost certainly the man most anguished by the storm was Frank Sinatra, the big show's impresario. Musical lead sheet in hand, Sinatra rehearsed the pure-platinum chorus he and Peter Lawford had assembled to help replenish the Democrats' $2 million deficit. Among the performers were (from left) Keely Smith, Nat King Cole, Harry Belafonte, Ella Fitzgerald, Alan King, Gene Kelly, Janet Leigh, Tony Curtis and Milton Berle. Others included Fredric March, who read Lincoln's pre-Inaugural address; Laurence Olivier, who delivered a British tribute; and Ethel Merman, a Republican who belted *Everything's Coming Up Roses.*

Though the weather outside was frightful, the armory show was a smash. The singing stars were matched by the dancers (above), who included young Juliet Prowse (above right). Tony Curtis and Janet Leigh (right, in the wings) were a husband-and-wife team. The gala made nearly $1.4 million. When the rest of the clan and their show-business buddies moved on to various bashes, Jackie went home but Jack joined them. It was 4 a.m. before he slipped into bed.

Before it ended, long after midnight, the big snowfall
deposited downy white cushions on the seats in
the reviewing stand (below) and coated the roofed section
from which Kennedy was to review the Inaugural parade.

Stellar by candlelight

Making a detour on his way to a family celebration, the President-to-be dropped in on the Washington Hilton party Sinatra flung for his stars. Among the luminaries in this picture, which Phil Stern made solely by the light of candles, are comedian Bill Dana and Gloria Cahn, wife of lyricist Sammy Cahn.

Goodbye, Mr. President
Good morning, Mr. President

When, one minute after 11 o'clock, J.F.K. was welcomed to his new home by his predecessor (above), his first words were, "Good morning, Mr. President." Because of the snow, the Eisenhowers had invited the Kennedys in for coffee before the swearing-in. Jack and Jackie drank in their surroundings (above, right) and then Ike ushered Jack to their waiting coffee and a brief tour of the executive offices (right). The morning interlude resolved doubts each of the men had about the other, and tensions between them noticeably lessened.

Earlier, President and Mamie Eisenhower, dressed for the ceremonies, took their leave of the White House service staff (far left). Then Ike went to the entrance and waited for his successor (left).

As thousands congealed

The temperature was 20°F as expectant Inaugural multitudes filled the Capitol plaza or sat, some wearing improvised face masks, in the stands. Heaters were placed along the balusters of the Inaugural platform (built to match the Captiol's architecture) but there were none in the huge press stand facing the microphone-equipped lectern that would be the center of the action. Three thousand servicemen had worked through the night with 700 plows and trucks to sweep the area clear of snow.

A moment of warmth

The arrival of the President-to-be at the swearing-in site, where President Eisenhower and Mamie, Chief Justice Earl Warren, the Nixons, Johnsons and other dignitaries waited, was the occasion for a round of handclapping that was warming in every sense of the word. Robert Kennedy (right), in the top hat that his brother had decreed proper for the occasion, savored the historic moment with a grin of satisfaction just short of triumphant.

I do
solemnly swear
that I will
faithfully
execute
the office of
President
of the
United States,
and will,
to the best
of my ability,
preserve,
protect,
and defend the
Constitution
of the
United States.
So help me God.

At the moment of oath
taking, the raised hands of
Earl Warren and John
Kennedy appeared
to frame the heads of
Jacqueline Kennedy and
Richard Nixon.

Let the word go forth from this time and place, to friend and foe alike

By the time the clear young voice with its now-familiar Cape Cod ring, had delivered three paragraphs of the new President's message, it was clear to his listeners that this would be one of the most memorable of Inaugural addresses.

No Kennedy speech had ever undergone so many drafts, according to Ted Sorensen, his chief speechwriter, who had helped him analyze past Inaugural addresses and Lincoln's Gettysburg Address. But as had been true throughout his political career, it was J.F.K. who was the principal architect of his speech. He started putting it together on paper in Palm Beach a week before Inauguration Day and made his last emendations on Jan. 19, the day before he delivered it.

We observe today not a victory of party but a celebration of freedom—symbolizing an end as well as a beginning—signifying renewal as well as change. For I have sworn before you and Almighty God the same solemn oath our forebears prescribed nearly a century and three-quarters ago.

The world is very different now. For man holds in his mortal hands the power to abolish all forms of human poverty and all forms of human life. And yet the same revolutionary beliefs for which our forebears fought are still at issue around the globe—the belief that the rights of man come not from the generosity of the state but from the hand of God.

We dare not forget today that we are the heirs of that first revolution. Let the word go forth from this time and place, to friend and foe alike, that the torch has been passed to a new generation of Americans—born in this century, tempered by war, disciplined by a hard and bitter peace, proud of our ancient heritage—and unwilling to witness or permit the slow undoing of those human rights to which this nation has al-

ways been committed, and to which we are committed today at home and around the world.

Let every nation know, whether it wishes us well or ill, that we shall pay any price, bear any burden, meet any hardship, support any friend, oppose any foe to assure the survival and the success of liberty.

This much we pledge—and more.

To those old allies whose cultural and spiritual origins we share, we pledge the loyalty of faithful friends. United, there is little we cannot do in a host of new cooperative ventures. Divided, there is little we can do—for we dare not meet a powerful challenge at odds and split asunder.

To those new states whom we welcome to the ranks of the free, we pledge our word that one form of colonial control shall not have passed away merely to be replaced by a far more iron tyranny. We shall not always expect to find them supporting our view. But we shall always hope to find them strongly supporting their own freedom—and to remember that, in the past, those who foolishly sought power by riding the back of the tiger ended up inside.

To those peoples in the huts and villages of half the globe struggling to break the bonds of mass misery, we pledge our best efforts to help them help themselves, for whatever period is required—not because the Communists may be doing it, not because we seek their votes, but because it is right. If a free society cannot help the many who are poor, it cannot save the few who are rich.

To our sister republics south of our border, we offer a special pledge—to convert our good words into good deeds—in a new alliance for progress—to assist free men and free governments in casting off the chains of poverty. But this peaceful revolu-

tion of hope cannot become the prey of hostile powers. Let all our neighbors know that we shall join with them to oppose aggression or subversion anywhere in the Americas. And let every other power know that this hemisphere intends to remain the master of its own house.

To that world assembly of sovereign states, the United Nations, our last best hope in an age

where the instruments of war have far outpaced the instruments of peace, we renew our pledge of support—to prevent it from becoming merely a forum for invective—to strengthen its shield of the new and the weak—and to enlarge the area in which its writ may run.

Finally, to those nations who

would make themselves our adversary, we offer not a pledge but a request: that both sides begin anew the quest for peace, before the dark powers of destruction unleashed by science engulf all humanity in planned or accidental self-destruction.

We dare not tempt them with weakness. For only when our arms are sufficient beyond doubt can we be certain beyond

doubt that they will never be employed.

But neither can two great and powerful groups of nations take comfort from our present course—both sides overburdened by the cost of modern weapons, both rightly alarmed by the steady spread of the deadly atom, yet both racing to

alter that uncertain balance of terror that stays the hand of mankind's final war.

So let us begin anew—remembering on both sides that civility is not a sign of weakness, and sincerity is always subject to proof. Let us never negotiate out of fear. But let us never fear to negotiate.

Let both sides explore what problems unite us instead of belaboring those problems which divide us.

Let both sides, for the first time, formulate serious and precise proposals for the inspection and control of arms—and bring the absolute power to destroy other nations under the absolute control of all nations.

Let both sides seek to invoke the wonders of science instead of its terrors. Together let us explore the stars, conquer the deserts, eradicate disease, tap the ocean depths and encourage the arts and commerce.

Let both sides unite to heed in all corners of the earth the command of Isaiah—to "undo the heavy burdens . . . [and] let the oppressed go free."

And if a beachhead of cooperation may push back the jungles of suspicion, let both sides join in creating a new endeavor—not a new balance of power, but a new world of law, where the strong are just and the weak secure and the peace preserved.

All this will not be finished in the first 100 days. Nor will it be finished in the first 1,000 days, nor in the lifetime of this Administration, nor even perhaps in our lifetime on this planet. But let us begin.

In your hands, my fellow citizens, more than mine, will rest the final success or failure of our course. Since this country was founded, each generation of Americans has been summoned to give testimony to its national loyalty. The graves of young

Americans who answered the call to service surround the globe.

Now the trumpet summons us again—not as a call to bear arms, though arms we need—not as a call to battle, though embattled we are—but a call to bear the burden of a long twilight struggle year in and year out, "rejoicing in hope, patient in tribulation"—a struggle against the common enemies of man: tyranny, poverty, disease and war itself.

Can we forge against these enemies a grand and global alliance, north and south, east and west, that can assure a more fruitful life for all mankind? Will you join in that historic effort?

In the long history of the world, only a few generations have been granted the role of defending freedom in its hour of maximum danger. I do not shrink from this responsibility—I welcome it. I do not believe that any of us would exchange places with any other people or any other generation. The energy, the faith, the devotion which we bring to this endeavor will light our country and all who serve it—and the glow from that fire can truly light the world.

And so, my fellow Americans: ask not what your country can do for you— ask what you can do for your country.

My fellow citizens of the world: ask not what America will do for you, but what together we can do for the freedom of man.

Finally, whether you are citizens of America or citizens of the world, ask of us here the same high standards of strength and sacrifice which we ask of you. With a good conscience our only sure reward, with history the final judge of our deeds, let us go forth to lead the land we love, asking His blessing and His help, but knowing that here on earth God's work must truly be our own.

No prouder parents ever heard a son's commencement speech

Rose and Joseph listened intently as their son,
still without the overcoat he had shed before
taking the oath, delivered his address.

A quartet of First Ladies

**All First Ladies of the past, present or future,
the front line of women, Pat Nixon, Mamie Eisenhower,**

Lady Bird Johnson and Jacqueline Kennedy, were studies in absorption during the address, as were, close behind them, Pat Lawford and Eunice Shriver.

"The land was ours before we were the land's"

Everyone was concerned for Robert Frost when the 86-year-old poet, dazzled by the sun on his wind-whipped script, faltered as he read a newly written dedication to his well-loved poem *The Gift Outright*. Johnson whipped forth his top hat for shade; Lady Bird, Jackie and Ike sat in vicarious anguish. "This was supposed to be a preface to a poem that I can say to you without seeing it," Frost went on. "The poem goes this way . . ." In the saying, he changed "will" to "would" in the last line.

THE GIFT OUTRIGHT

The land was ours before we were the land's.
She was our land more than a hundred years
Before we were her people. She was ours
In Massachusetts, in Virginia,
But we were England's, still colonials,
Possessing what we still were unpossessed by,
Possessed by what we now no more possessed.
Something we were withholding made us weak
Until we found out that it was ourselves
We were withholding from our land of living.
And forthwith found salvation in surrender.
Such as we were we gave ourselves outright
(The deed of gift was many deeds of war)
To the land vaguely realizing westward.
But still unstoried, artless, unenhanced,
Such as she was, such as she will become.

The brand-new President tried out the seat of power

Even before taking his place at the head of the Inauguration parade, Kennedy repaired to the virtually bare Oval Office and sat at the big desk. He never did get over his small boy's awe at working and living in the White House.

The President and the [First] Lady led off the Inaugural parade, rid[ing] as far as the White House in a car (left) th[at] was, like J.F.K. himself, uncovered. Joining L.[B.J.] in the reviewing stand[s]

The procession continued marching down
Pennsylvania Avenue long after dark.

ove, he was moved to
e an unprecedented
his father rose on
rrival. J.F.K.
ed down hot coffee
then stood up at
ail to watch the
of the parade.

They marched into the night

The scene in the 2½-acre National Guard Armory as the President and his First Lady entered was truly fit for a king and queen. Four other balls took place in hotel ballrooms; Kennedy appeared at all of them and never appeared winded.

Ruffles, flourishes and a sense of unbuttoned fun

The presidential box at the armory bash was the focus of thousands of dancing couples. They saw both comedy and drama there. When Joe Kennedy removed his overcoat with a flourish, he also removed his tails.

Jackie, the silver embroidery of her white satin Bergdorf sheath showing through a sheer overblouse, drew aahs and a flurry of applause as she was conducted to her seat.

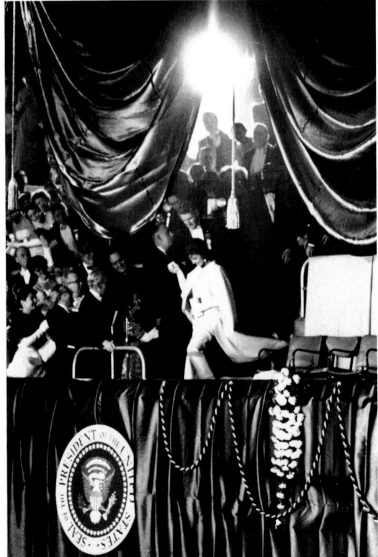

A dancer could hardly whirl his partner around the dance floor without brushing some notable, such as United Auto Workers chief Walter Reuther. Jackie sat this one out (left) with her own pick of the VIPs.

The Kennedy imprint began to show

As the exuberance mounted, one of the guests, in top hat, white tie and tails, cut a figure that was as much Kennedy as Astaire.

Presiding over the ball, J.F.K. was surrounded by family and friends. His mother and father sat at his right. On his left were Jacqueline, Vice President Johnson, Lady Bird and the two Johnson daughters, Lynda Bird and Lucy. Jackie flagged as the night wore on. She left at midnight—not losing either of her slippers—but her prince dropped in on all four other balls, plus a party at the Georgetown home of columnist Joe Alsop. He kept going until around 4 a.m.

"Renewal as well as change"

A 1956 sedan turned up a snowy Pennsylvania lane and Dwight Eisenhower, who just that morning had governed the world's most powerful nation, was home on his Gettysburg farm, a private citizen. Back in the Washington armory, his young successor savored the moment even as he relished the challenge of the future. Hours before, he had said, "I do not believe that any of us would exchange places with any other people of any other generation."

Chapter 11

THE GOOD TIMES

"When power leads man toward arrogance, poetry reminds him of his limitations. When power narrows the areas of man's concern, poetry reminds him of the richness and

The winds of change, in Harold Macmillan's felicitously timed phrase, swept through the U.S. with the advent of J.F.K.'s administration. It stirred first and most noticeably in the White House, which soon had not just a new look but also a new sound, a new feeling, as the new President and his wife indulged their shared enthusiasm for the arts. J.F.K. assembled a Cabinet of thinkers and doers that he hoped would be an unprecedented ministry of talent. Kennedy's White House visitors tended to be artists, writers, musicians. When Pablo Casals, 85, played at a dinner honoring Puerto Rico governor Luis Muñoz Marin (at right), it was the first time Casals had set foot in the White House since 1904 when he played for Teddy Roosevelt. Jackie, surprised to find that the Executive Mansion's furnishings and decor failed to live up to its history, refurbished it and turned it into a showplace. Jack, similarly distressed to discover that the Rose Garden had become a weedy, shrub-constricted enclave, had the ground plowed up and turned into an 18th century garden with a velvet lawn. The passion for improvement, intellectual and physical, at home and abroad, was contagious. The era of the cultural center dawned. New York City opened the first buildings of Lincoln Center. The Peace Corps came into being and spread round the world. The hardworking, hard-playing Kennedys put their imprint on a society eager for a change.

diversity of his existence. When power corrupts, poetry cleanses. For art establishes the basic human truths which must serve as the touchstones of our judgment."

Pablo Casals bowed to the delighted applause of the Kennedys, their guests of honor, Puerto Rico governor Luis Munoz Marin and his wife, and other White House guests. At Jackie's left was Senora Casals.

The proud proprietor showed the Netherlands' Princess Beatrix through the refurbished Rose Garden.

Plants are keyed to numbers on the beds below by general species only, although some include several varieties. Here are 1) the herb echinops; 2) tulips; 3) Saunders hybrid peonies; 4) anemones; 5) roses; 6) santolina; 7) heliotrope; 8) the mint nepeta; 9) lady's-mantle; 10) columbine; 11) white violas; 12) dianthus; 13) grape hyacinths.

Blossom time at the White House

The Rose Garden, which he rebuilt from scratch, was J.F.K.'s proudest showcase for visiting VIPs. He and Jackie had persuaded an old friend, Mrs. Paul Mellon, an amateur landscape architect, to redesign the rundown 50-year-old garden to 1) provide more lawn area for shmoozing and 2) flower during a larger part of the year. This she accomplished by pruning back overgrown shrubs, planting a completely new lawn of state-of-the-art Merion bluegrass and framing it with a flower border right out of the 18th century. The floral plan at right shows how one section of the border achieved its protracted bloom.

e timing of the Dutch Princess's
it was most appropriate, as
e garden blazed with many of
e bulbs from her country,
cluding these tulips beneath
flowering crab-apple tree.

So much to do in only a thousand days

Peace Corps volunteers said goodbye to President Kennedy at a White House reception before their departure for Ghana and Tanganyika.

Signing the last milestone document of his career, the hard-won nuclear test-ban treaty of 1963, the President handed out the pens he had used for his signature to members of the Senate Foreign Relations Committee. From left, Secretary of State Dean Rusk, John O. Pastore (D-R.I.), Howard W. Cannon (D-Nev.), Leverett Saltonstall (R-Mass.), Thomas H. Kuchel (R-Calif.) and Vice President Johnson.

From the Bay of Pigs to the test-ban treaty

When John Kennedy flew to Cape Canaveral to pin a medal on Lieutenant Colonel John Glenn for making the first orbital flight in U.S. history, he was celebrating Step No. 2 (Navy Commander Alan Shepard's suborbital flight was No. 1) in the march to the fulfillment of his early pledge to place a U.S. space team on the moon before 1970. This was the boldest of the challenge-meeting actions he took in the "thousand days" that were to be his allotted term. But other actions he took rivaled it in nobility of purpose. Two months into his administration (the same month in which he accepted responsibility for the Bay of Pigs landing), he created, by executive action, the Peace Corps, which recruited young Americans to serve as ambassadors of peace to foreign countries. He also launched the Alliance for Progress to strengthen the bonds between the U.S. and Latin America.

Between these early flights of creativity and the capstone accomplishment of his career, the nuclear test-ban treaty of 1963, J.F.K. had, among other things, retained Western access to Berlin in the face of Soviet threats by increasing combat forces; pressured the steel industry to rescind its announced price increases; imposed a quarantine to force the U.S.S.R. to remove its missiles from Cuba; sped aid to India under attack from Red China; sent troops to enforce court-ordered desegregation at the University of Mississippi and met with the leaders of the Washington March in support of his proposals on civil rights.

At Cape Canaveral, J.F.K. and earth orbiter John Glenn joined in a thumbs-up-to-the-moon salute.

Perks of office for a sports-loving First Fan

All that softball and association football at clan gatherings served the President in good stead when he threw out the first ball at the Washington Senators' opening game of the 1961 season, against the Chicago White Sox. He was the best pitcher from the White House since Teddy Roosevelt.

Although the Commander in Chief was a Navy man, the ex-skipper of *PT-109* applauded good plays by both teams as he watched the 1962 Army-Navy football game at Franklin Field in Philadelphia. He switched sides at halftime, as a President should.

The Kennedy image was everywhere, from sea to shining sea

Wherever one looked in the U.S., there were Jack and/or Jackie on every hand. Or, sometimes, on every face. The latest technology in beauty products, plastic masks of a material that screened out harmful ultraviolet rays and admitted those that tanned, caused beaches to bloom with their likenesses. They came in eight colors—the deeper the shade the lighter the tan.

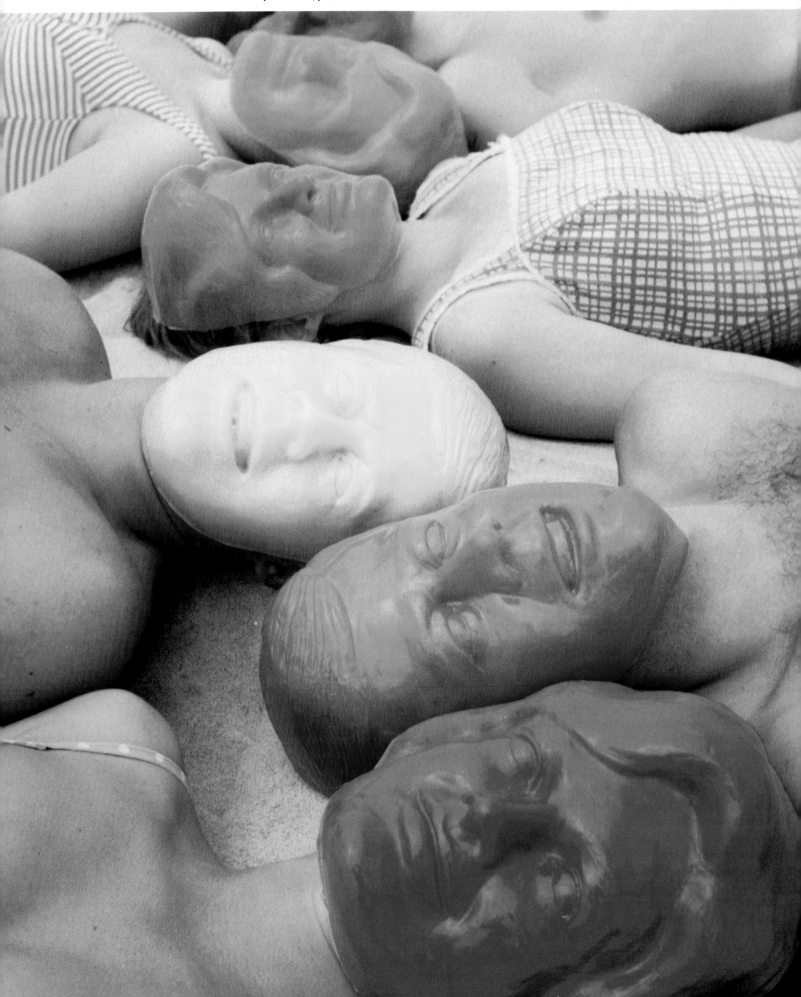

Cliff Robertson, after a head hunt for a Kennedy look-alike, was chosen (with J.F.K.'s approval) to play the skipper in *PT-109,* Warner Brothers' film version of Kennedy's war heroism.

Vaughn Meader, who devoted his professional life to duplicating J.F.K.'s voice and mannerisms, was the most successful of a horde of TV and nightclub carbon-copy Kennedys.

Not just Kennedy faces but Kennedy figures proliferated as well. Jack and Jacqueline mannequins drew stares in many a store window, and even more, as here in New York, en route.

Mrs. Kennedy's celebrated fashion sense also benefited living, breathing mannequins, such as (from left) Jackie doubles Jeani Kitchens, Joanne Hilem, Dorothea McCarthy and Eugenia McLin.

Like mother, like daughter. Jackie at age 10 dressed up as an Indian maid and rode her piebald pony, Dance Step, in a horse show. Caroline, 4 (below), didn't stick a feather in her impeccable riding cap but she did call her pony Macaroni and she rode him with blue-ribbon style on her Uncle Bobby's McLean, Virginia, estate.

In Camelot even a fall could look good

Even in her bad moments, the First Lady was a class act. When her mount, a bay gelding named Bit of Irish, refused to jump a split-rail fence during a fox hunt on Paul Mellon's Virginia estate (right), Jacqueline continued on, with consummate grace. Picking herself up, she promptly remounted and rode on.

"Happy birthday, dear Mr. President, happy birthday to you"

The 45-candle birthday cake got a round of applause when it was presented to the birthday boy at the Madison Square Garden fund raiser 10 days before J.F.K.'s birthday in 1962. But it couldn't hold a candle to the gasp that greeted Marilyn Monroe when, approaching the mike to sing *Happy Birthday* to the Chief, she whipped off her white mink and revealed what for one brief, shining moment appeared to be nothing at all. It turned out to be a skin-tight, flesh-toned creation by Hollywood costume designer Jean-Louis, embroidered with rhinestones and with "nothing," as he later confided to the press, "absolutely nothing, underneath." M.M. gave a little-girl ("sweet, wholesome," J.F.K. called it) rendition, getting all the syllables of *"Happy birthday, dear Mr. President"* into the third line without a bobble. It was some years later that gossip started circulating about secret trysts between her and Jack.

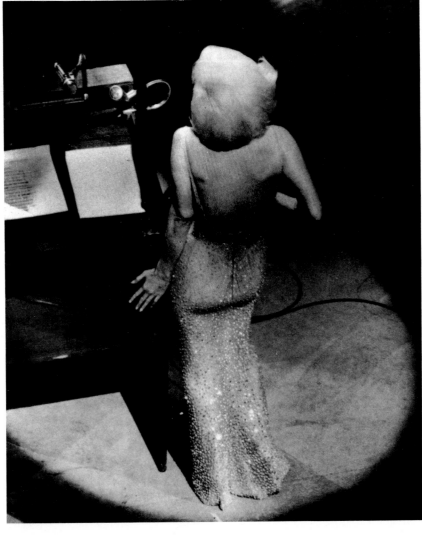

In the Manhattan town house of United Artists president Arthur Krim, to which the celebrants repaired for a more exclusive bash, the President and brother Bobby chatted with the actress. Fellow guest Adlai Stevenson said she was "dressed in what she calls 'skin and beads,'" and added, "I didn't see the beads."

Culture and glamour melded as the First Lady, in a rustle of satin, greeted maestro Leonard Bernstein (left) at the most elegant musical event of the century, the 1962 opening of New York's glittering Philharmonic Hall. It was the first act of a production that was to become the 14-acre, six-building Lincoln Center for the Performing Arts.

Jackie smiled back at Leonard Bernstein and the Mona Lisa

Cultural Minister Andre Malraux conversed animatedly in French with Jacqueline at the National Gallery. He had just opened the exhibition, largely the result of her interest in art, of "the most famous painting in the world," Leonardo's *Mona Lisa* (far right), on loan from France. Posed against the burgundy backdrop that matched the portrait's Louvre wall were Jackie, flanked by M. and Mme. Malraux, the President, Secretary of State Rusk and the first lady of the Louvre, officially known as *La Gioconda.*

A pair of lissome listeners (LIFE likened them to bending birches) leaned to catch the words of Robert Frost after dinner.

As the evening drew toward its end, the host, his hand on Jackie's shoulder, chatted with guests, including (at left) writer Pearl Buck.

A Jeffersonian collection of talent

"I think this is the most extraordinary collection of talent, of human knowledge . . . ever gathered at the White House, with the possible exception of when Thomas Jefferson dined alone," President Kennedy told 175 dinner guests in May 1962, when he was host to 49 Nobel laureates and other cognoscenti. Illustrating his thesis—and perhaps some corollary concerning the nature of American democracy—1954 Nobel-winning chemist Linus C. Pauling whirled his wife around the marble floor of the main hallway (below); the two previous days he had picketed the Executive Mansion to protest the U.S. resumption of nuclear testing. Later in the year he won the Nobel Peace Prize to become the first recipient of the award in two categories.

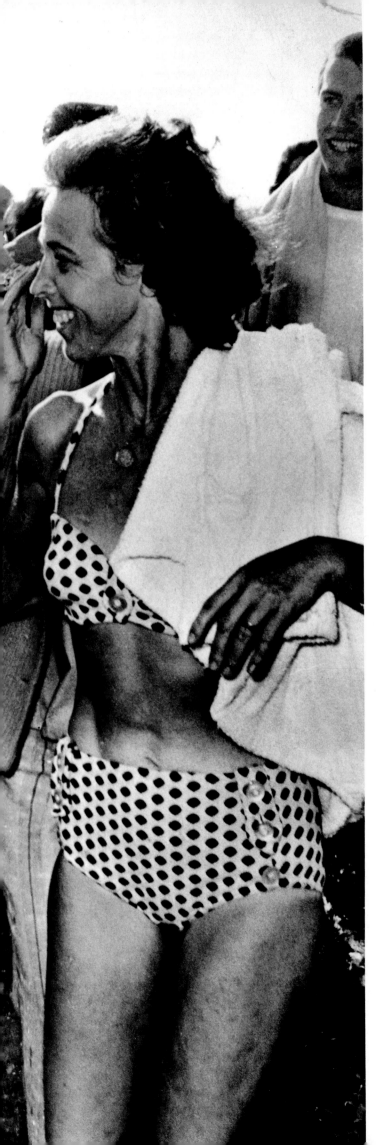

Images from the world press's "Only in America" department

Princess Grace of Monaco, the former movie star Grace Kelly, whose generational progression from Irish immigrant forebears to the realization of storybook dreams strikingly reflected the Kennedy saga, looked appreciatively upon her host during a White House visit with her husband, Prince Rainier. Her turban was her solution to a coiffure crisis.

The First Lady, America's No. 1 French connection, usually more debonair with champagne, splashily christened the Polaris sub U.S.S. *Lafayette* at Groton, Connecticut. Said the former Miss Bouvier: "*Je te baptise Lafayette.*"

While Jackie was off on the Italian Riviera giving the paparazzi a field day, the President, on a "nonpolitical" swing through the West, waded into the surf at Santa Monica, California, making the day of the beach-blanket set and, in a different sense, of the Secret Service.

Christenings, birthdays, holidays, parties for all occasions filled the family album, a record of the Kennedys' self-contained baby boom

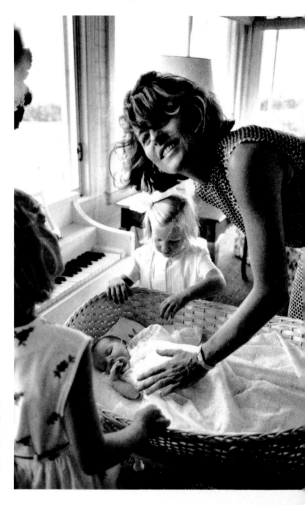

Godmother Pat Lawford bent over the bassinet of Christopher George Kennedy, Ethel and Bobby's eighth, before his christening at Hyannis, Massachusetts, in the summer of 1963.

Pat held her nephew as Richard Cardinal Cushing read the baptismal service in St. Francis Xavier Church. Beside her stood Christopher's godfather, Dean Markham, the head of the President's Committee on Narcotics and Drug Abuse. The President stationed himself off on the left flank next to his brother. He admitted that Christopher "looks like a good baby. But," he added judiciously, "of course, we'll know more later."

ddy, the Attorney General,
tted daughter Kerry, 3,
th the long arms of the law.

When R.F.K. saw Ethel holding Christopher in his christening gown, he cracked, "Holy mackerel, Ethel, you've done it again!"

After the ceremony, its little star made his debut on the church steps in the arms of his godmother, amid an exaltation of Kennedy kids and buddies. The grownups who got into the act were (from left) Robert Kennedy, President Kennedy, Cardinal Cushing, Ethel Kennedy and Dean Markham.

The day John Jr. turned one

LIFE's Mark Shaw, having become the official White House photographer, was setting up his lights in the Oval Office to make an official first-birthday portrait of John Jr. when he heard Caroline noises from the First Daughter's nearby bedroom. He crossed the corridor and snapped Caroline hiding out from her kid brother (right). He went right on shooting unprecedented pictures, with the assistance of big sis, who enthusiastically kept hoisting the 23-pounder to his feet for "just one more" (bottom picture). Then Shaw went back to the Oval Office and took the official portrait (below) of J.F.K. Jr. munching on a birthday toy from Charles de Gaulle.

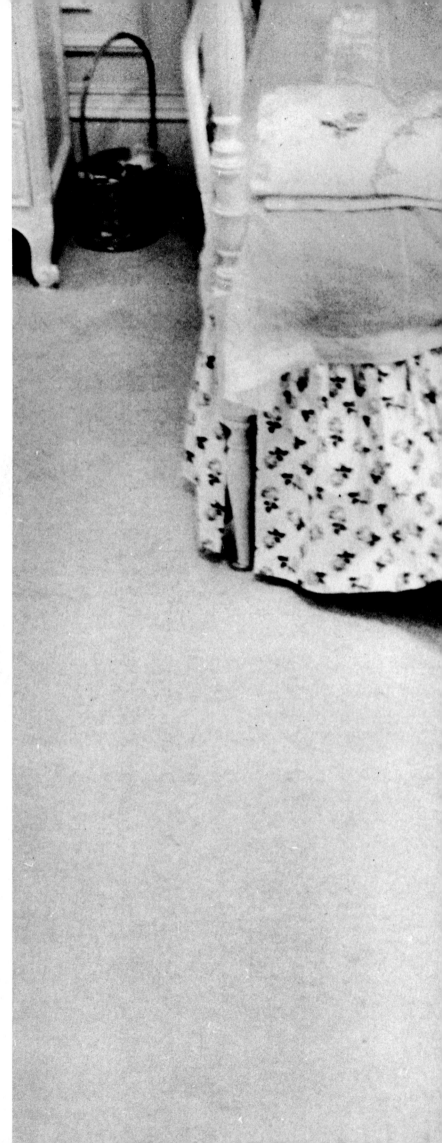

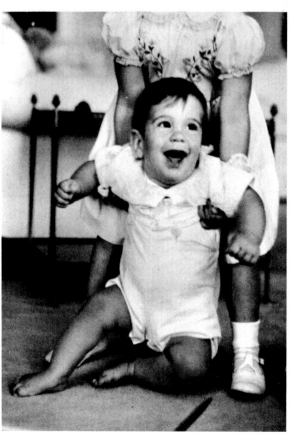

Halloween in the Oval Office

One dark and spooky
night, the last night
of October 1963, the
Oval Office was invaded
by the awfulest of
witches and the goofiest
of clowns. The late-
working occupant was
relieved and
delighted to learn that
they were relatives of his.

. . . or mulling a major decision whose effect might influence the lives of millions. He kept no rigid schedule, Schutzer found, but applied himself directly to whatever needed doing at the moment.

study by Paul Schutzer of the
esident's expressions and moods in
e course of a 1961 working day
vealed a characteristic that J.F.K.
dmired in F.D.R. He kept his undivided
ttention on the task at hand, be it
nall and pleasurable, like helping
aroline avoid stepping on cracks en
ute along the East Wing
olonnade . . .

He loved his family and liked to contemplate the future

Chapter 12

CAMELOT HAD ITS BAD MOMENTS

"Today, every inhabitant of this planet must contemplate the day when it may no longer be habitable. Every man, woman, and child lives under a nuclear sword of Damocles, hanging by the slenderest of threads, capable of being cut at any moment . . . by accident, miscalculation or madness. The weapons of war must be abolished before they abolish us."

Five days after the abortive invasion, President Kennedy and former President Eisenhower met at Camp David, the effect of the failure written on their faces. Castro's photographers pictured Cuban militiamen (below) with Czech-made rifles battling a thrust by invaders some 10 miles inland from the landing site on the island's south coast.

The idyll was shattered early on. On April 17, 1961, with J.F.K.'s reluctant approval, some 1,300 members of an anti-Communist Cuban exile force landed in the Zapata Swamp at Cuba's Bay of Pigs. This military brigade had been raised in 1960 at President Eisenhower's direction, and armed and trained in Guatemala by the CIA. Because providing U.S. air cover "would have meant a full-fledged invasion" by the U.S., Kennedy withheld it. Within two days Castro crushed the invasion.

J.F.K. accepted responsibility for the disaster. He had never had illusions that any presidency

could be crisis-free, but he admitted that the briefings he received after his election (as opposed to those he got as a candidate) "staggered" him. In the three months before the Cuban fiasco, these crises had appeared, among others: on March 9 he received detailed plans for introducing forces into Laos, which was on the verge of a Communist takeover—a foreshadowing of the fateful involvement in Vietnam; on March 18, NATO ally Portugal rushed troops into Angola to put down a nationalist uprising supported by African nations friendly to the U.S.; on March 21 the Soviets

made a new demand for a U.N. veto over all inspection, dimming hope for nuclear disarmament—something close to his heart—and on April 12 the U.S.S.R. orbited the first man in space.

Other crises followed, the greatest one in October 1962, when nuclear missile sites appeared in Cuba and for one week the world feared nuclear war was at hand.

The most painful domestic problems were inflation and the continuing crisis in integration. The violence that erupted in Oxford when James Meredith enrolled in the University of Missis-

sippi so concerned the President that he personally engineered the moves of federal marshals and U.S. troops who fended off student and local mobs.

The most dangerous challenge to his efforts to combat inflation was the threat of a price increase by the steel industry, and it simmered for a full year before it produced a dramatic confrontation between Kennedy and U.S. Steel. In April 1962, U.S. Steel and then the rest of Big Steel announced the increase. J.F.K. brought all the force of the government to bear on the industry, and 72 hours later the price hike was rescinded.

The Oval Office was the command post for two battlefronts—integration and inflation

The 24 federal marshals assigned to protect James Meredith when he registered for classes at Ole Miss were attacked and besieged by armed mobs. The rioters were not restrained by Mississippi plainclothesmen (right), who had in fact mobilized to help them. One practiced his swing with the billy that would teach those "nigger lovers" a lesson. When the rioting broke out, they vamoosed. The next morning, Monday, Meredith, gasping from residual tear gas (below, right) headed for his first class, surrounded by marshals and federal troops. When National Guard troops (below), brought in to beef up the outnumbered and outgunned federal marshals, sought permission to return the mob's fire, Deputy U.S. Attorney General Nicholas Katzenbach replied, "If you can hold your fire for a few minutes more, the President is on the telephone talking to the governor [Ross Barnett] now." No shots were fired by the federal side.

The President spent an inordinate amount of time on the phone (far right). Earlier in the year, during his three-day war against Big Steel, he was constantly in communication with Attorney General Bobby and other field commanders. Inflation—his other great priority—stemmed directly from steel prices. While R.F.K.'s Justice Department investigated whether simultaneous and identical price increases violated the Sherman Anti-Trust Act, the Defense Department moved to shift orders to small independents and alternative materials. The rescission of the increase yielded the first steel settlement without a strike since 1954, one that was within the bounds of increased productivity.

Red missiles in Cuba: a classic case of crisis management

When, on the morning of Oct. 16, 1962, President Kennedy got the news that aerial photos showed evidence of nuclear offensive missiles in Cuba, he reacted, quite normally, with a few epithets and a declaration that armed forces would have to remove the threat. But even as the emotional adrenaline surge subsided, J.F.K. made his intellect take over. He recast the challenge as one of communication, not warfare, and throughout the heat of the crisis he never let it get out of that realm.

"He set his course by his sense of history," Hugh Sidey wrote later, "a kind of inner road map warning him of human misjudgment and prejudice." He sought to see things from Khrushchev's side. If J.F.K. presumed war was inevitable, would that not also be the Soviet leader's initial reasoning?

Despite pressure from Congress and the press for air strikes or invasion, he ordered a blockade of Cuba, not to interdict missiles (belatedly) but to send Khrushchev a message—couched in moderate language—of U.S. determination. To give the U.S.S.R. hours more to think, he reduced the perimeter from 800 to 500 miles. (History vindicated his moderation. A joint 1987 conference of U.S. and Soviet officials who had taken part in the 1962 confrontation decided Khrushchev had installed the missile sites without giving much thought to U.S. reaction.)

Kennedy got the Soviets to remove the missile sites, ending the brush with nuclear war, by responding reasonably to an opening in one of two invective-filled Khrushchev letters. He pledged not to invade Cuba, in return for the U.S.S.R.'s withdrawing of the missiles; the later official letter from Moscow, raising the ante, was ignored.

During the crisis, while not only America but all the world waited in dread of nuclear war, President Kennedy and his brother stepped outside the White House to meet Secretary of State Rusk, arriving with his dispatch case, and Special Assistant McGeorge Bundy with his arms full of papers.

The President was grave but forthright on television when he told the country about the Soviet missiles in Cuba, denouncing the Soviets' "deliberate deception." The picture at right, one of several that were dramatically displayed at the U.N., showed clearly the extent of the Soviet missile installations. It was made from a low-flying U.S. reconnaissance plane. The annotations were by Defense Department experts. This was the Sagua la Grande missile site, 218 miles from Havana. Two launchpads were operational, capable of launching missiles with a range of up to 1,200 miles. Tracks indicated one or more missiles were inside the ready buildings.

LAUNCH PAD WITH ERECTOR

CABLING

Pictures that told the whole chilling story of the missile buildup

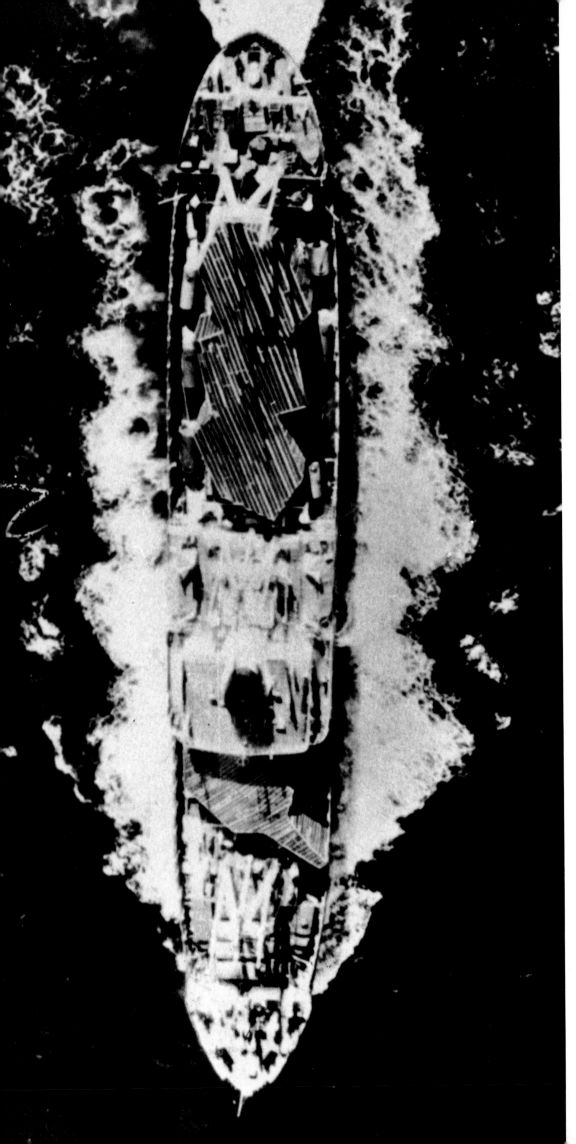

The weapons that had brought the threat of war departed

Aerial photography, which had stirred fear when it revealed a Havana-bound shipload (left) of warplanes (fuselages along the rails, complete planes, presumably bombers, in the big slatted crates) had the opposite effect when its object was a ship departing Cuba with a cargo of shrouded missile launchers (below).

Even as the ships carried missiles away, Khrushchev, in Moscow, appeared shaken (below). Not so Castro, who in Havana listened, with his lieutenants, in disdain as U Thant (in glasses) argued for a U.N. watch over the dismantling of the missile sites.

A recurrence of J.F.K.'s old back trouble added to his problems

Wielding a shovel at a tree-planting ceremony in Canada, Kennedy strained his lower back muscles, bringing back his 1937 football injury and sending him off to recuperate in Palm Beach. He was boosted into Air Force One by a cherry picker (below) like the one that had lifted Alan Shepard into his rocket, and helped on the ground by a good old-fashioned pair of crutches.

The effects of the President's aching back weren't all bad. LIFE ran a piece showing him relaxing and enjoying himself in his favorite therapeutic appliance— and soon everybody was buying rocking chairs, to the benefit of the furniture industry, interior designers and antiques dealers.

The country shared the President's vigil for his doomed baby son

A distraught Kennedy rode an elevator in Boston's Children's Hospital to the room (right) where doctors and nurses bent over Patrick Bouvier Kennedy, born that morning by caesarean section. The baby, five weeks premature and weighing but four pounds 10 ounces, could not overcome the lung ailment not uncommon in

such cases, despite the finest medical care and the nation's prayers. J.F.K., happy
with his White House kids, had looked forward with special pleasure to Patrick's
arrival. "He wouldn't take his hands off that little coffin," said Cardinal Cushing, who
conducted the mass. "I was afraid he'd carry it right out with him."

Chapter 13

WOWING THE WORLD

"The United States will risk its cities to defend yours because we need your freedom to protect ours"

John Kennedy had always been more deeply interested in foreign affairs than in domestic problems. The big difference between the two, he observed early on, "is between a bill being defeated and the country being wiped out." As heir to F.D.R.'s Good Neighbor policy, J.F.K. launched the idea of the Alliance for Progress right in his Inaugural Address, and saw to it that his first trip outside the U.S. was to Canada. He followed up quickly with a transatlantic thrust, to the France of Charles de Gaulle, who was grumping that the NATO alliance threatened France's primacy, to a Vienna meeting with Nikita Khrushchev, and to Harold Macmillan's Britain.

Having boned up on De Gaulle's *Memoirs,* he disarmed the General ("I have more confidence in your country now," De Gaulle told him after they talked) even as Jacqueline was captivating the civilian population. (This was the occasion for his famous quote: "I am the man who accompanied Jacqueline Kennedy to Paris and I have enjoyed it.") He then conveyed the joint Franco-American message to Khrushchev: that both would fight, if necessary, to save Berlin.

Europe and Latin America—and no less other parts of the world—loved his style in communication as much as it adored Jackie's in fashion. He referred to the Communists not as evil, not as enemies, but as adversaries. In 1963, on the last, triumphal tour of his presidency to Western Europe and particularly to the Berlin Wall *("Ich bin ein Berliner"),* he reiterated the U.S. commitment to NATO: "Those who would separate Europe from America or split one ally from another would only give aid and comfort to men who make themselves our adversaries and welcome any Western disarray."

Kennedy and De Gaulle rode in pomp and splendor down Paris boulevards.

J.F.K. weathered a downpour of *papel* riding through Mexico City on a July 1962 state visit. He and Jackie had honeymooned in Mexico nine years before.

Hands across the border

The bilingual U.S. First Lady (left), the ideal state guest for bilingual Canada, joined her husband in planting symbolic trees on the grounds of Government House in Ottawa. She dug daintily; he hefted 10 spadefuls (which caused a recurrence of his old back problem). The purpose of his visit was to urge Prime Minister John Diefenbaker to join him in strengthening ties with Latin America. Canada was not yet a member of the Organization of American States.

The wooing of Charles de Gaulle

As De Gaulle welcomed the new young President to France (left), both were a bit like fencers *en garde.* Kennedy knew the General was wary of what he saw as "the Anglo-Saxons'" threat to France's supremacy on the Continent. At the Versailles reception dinner J.F.K., fascinated by De Gaulle's role in history, quizzed him about his peers. (Whom did he prefer, F.D.R. or Churchill? "I quarreled violently and bitterly with Churchill but always got on with him. I never quarreled with Roosevelt and never got on with him.") By the visit's end, the General had warmed visibly to his guest. As for Jacqueline, De Gaulle, a Frenchman after all, had no coolness to overcome; from the moment he escorted her to lunch in the Elysée Palace, he kept making gallant references to her graciousness, and even worked his admiration into his speeches.

Tales from the Vienna woods

De Gaulle may have got it backward in warning Mrs. Kennedy about Mrs. Khrushchev and Jack. It was *Mr.* Khrushchev who appeared smitten in the City of the Waltz. At a banquet he edged his chair closer to Jackie's and, eyes twinkling, told her funny stories.

J.F.K. carried to Latin America his passion for his *Alianza*; his dream of *Progreso* came more slowly

Visiting the Venezuelan capital of Caracas to push his Alliance for Progress, less than four years after Vice President Nixon had been endangered by rioters, Kennedy was received by cheering throngs (above and far right) like those he had encountered on his campaign tours. He had got Congress to appropriate funds for his 10-point "expression of the noblest goals of our society" but was staggered by the obstacles: high birth rate and infant mortality, low literacy and production, and above all the fact that 2 percent of the citizenry owned more than half the wealth. At right, he prayed in the Cathedral of San José, Costa Rica, during a conference of Latin American leaders. He had requested the convocation to discuss curbing the export of arms, agents and subversion from Cuba.

Visiting India without the President, Mrs. Kennedy sat with
her sister Lee Radziwell in an elaborately carved
howdah as they rode a painted elephant trumpeting pachyderm
ruffles and flourishes. Officially she enjoyed the rocking ride,
but her personal reaction leaked a couple of days later when
the President told an audience back home that his roving
ambassadress had had "her first—and last—ride on an elephant."

Jackie, on her own in India, was a diplomatic triumph

Jackie's rapture over the Taj Mahal was no diplomatic effusion. Experiencing it as below, in the morning light, thrilled her so much that she returned in moonlight to stand in awe before its pale splendor. Indians, smitten, showered her with gifts, and before she left for home she was *Ameriki Rani,* Queen of America.

Standing beside President Ayub Khan in an open car, Jacqueline beamed at crowds lining the way from the airport at Lahore. Before she flew off to London and luncheon with Queen Elizabeth, she had seen the Shalimar gardens, the Khyber Pass, Rawalpindi and Karachi. She, LIFE reported, charmed Pakistanis with the grace and sensitivity of her responses to everything she saw.

¡Bienvenido! south of the border

Navigating seas of sombreros, weathering storms of *¡olé!s,* graciously accepting a floral tribute from a noticeably awed admirer, Kennedy made his triumphant way through Mexico City. It was a visit calculated to get Mexico's President Lopez Mateos to endorse the *Alianza* and condemn Castro. *El Presidente's* reaction: the former *si,* the latter *no.*

"Barnstorming" for European unity

The first stop on Kennedy's 1963 journey to promote the Atlantic Alliance was Eire. It was chilly and windy (especially in his chopper's downblast) at the Galway Airport (far left) but warm and sunny in the hearts of his grandfather's countrymen. At Dunganstown in County Wexford, which he had visited 16 years previously, he got cookies and tea (and a kiss) from his third cousin Mary Ryan, 61 (center), who outranked the dozen or so other relatives he met on a lightning visit. In Dublin he laid a wreath (left) at the monument to those who died in the 1916 Easter Uprising.

The weather was better and the crowds were just as warm (left) at London's Gatwick Airport, J.F.K.'s next stop. On Sunday, Kennedy attended mass in the village of Forest Row, near the home of his host, Harold Macmillan. After church, he returned to Macmillan's residence for private talks with the PM.

A couple of generations of Berliners (one old enough to appreciate the delectable irony) welcomed the Americans to their city.

"Ich bin ein Berliner"

Kennedy fever reached its peak in Berlin. Police lines buckled as crowds surged forward to touch the President, or at least his car. At one point a couple of women got past security guards to grasp the hand of the highly receptive J.F.K., to the amusement of Mayor Willy Brandt and Chancellor Konrad Adenauer. The air in the former capital was electric.

Kennedy, never happy to be completely at rest, kept his fingers in motion (panel below) as he waited to deliver a speech. Finally, at Berlin's city hall, the familiar Boston voice carried over a vast sea of faces: "Two thousand years ago the proudest boast was *'Civis Romanus sum.'* Today, in the world of freedom, the proudest boast is *'Ich bin ein Berliner.'*"

History in Rome: the first Catholic U.S. President met a Pope

To cap his heady mission to Europe, Kennedy flew over the Alps to a meeting with the newly crowned Pope Paul VI. America's Chief Executive and the spiritual leader of his church talked privately in the Pontiff's library for 40 minutes. Paul praised the

President for his work in civil rights, peace and space exploration, and the two exchanged small gifts. Among them was a medallion of the Madonna and Child for the soon expected Kennedy baby.

Chapter 14

"We're really in 'nut' country now."

ASSASSINATION

In November of 1963, J.F.K. was at the height of his confidence. The U.S. was "stronger than ever before," he proclaimed, "and the possibilities of peace brighter . . ." The nation was prosperous, and under his leadership it had begun to confront its greatest moral and social problem—black equality. Recently, Kennedy had said that the rewards he found in his job were those of the Greek definition of happiness: "The full use of your powers along lines of excellence." Content in his marriage, healthier at 46 than he had ever been in his life, growing constantly in wisdom, undiscouraged that much of his program was stalled in Congress, Kennedy now began turning his attention to a second term. High on the agenda was a trip to Texas. A successful visit to such hostile territory— "nut" country he was to call it— would not only rally new support but it would also raise much-needed funds for his party. Texas Governor John Connally, who had served Kennedy as Secretary of the Navy, was put in charge of the trip. A crowded, two-day schedule of speeches, receptions, dinners and motorcades in the state's five most important cities was planned. Dallas was next to last. Triumphantly at midday, the President entered the city, and the city turned out handsomely to welcome him. And then he was dead. Suddenly, how suddenly, gone were the style and excitement. The fourth assassination of an American President in less than a century shook the world with shock and sorrow. And once again the nation's history was bloodied and disfigured.

With an hour to live, J.F.K., smiling, tanned and bareheaded, was greeted with enthusiasm at Dallas' Love Field. The early-morning clouds had lifted and a sparkling day seemed to predict immense success for this leg of the Texas visit.

His last morning alive started like so many others— with crowds, speeches and plenty of handshakes

On Friday morning after addressing the Fort Worth Chamber of Commerce at breakfast, Kennedy was happily assaulted by well-wishers in the parking lot across from the Texas Hotel. When told that Senator Yarborough had refused to ride in Vice President Johnson's car the day before because of a long-standing feud between the Texans, the President replied sharply, "I'll tell you one thing. He'll ride with him today or walk."

In Fort Worth it drizzled on his last morning of life, but the President stepped outside anyway, for a quick handshake with a horseman.

His final public prayer . . .

A last hand for Jackie . . .

His final speech was "strong and laced with a pleasant touch of fun," remembered Connally. With San Antonio, Houston and Fort Worth behind him, he was off for the short hop to Dallas.

As the Kennedys landed in Dallas, an unwatched FBI suspect was on the job filling orders at the downtown Book Depository

With roses in her arms and smiles for everyone, Jacqueline Kennedy still had one hour to share the buoyant surge of life with the man at her side. The motorcade into the heart of Dallas was about to begin. A city of "unpredictable madness," Adlai Stevenson had called it less than a month before, after having been struck and spat upon following a speech on the U.N. In 1960 even Lyndon Johnson had got the same

treatment (from rabid Nixon supporters), and that very morning an ugly advertisement had run in the Dallas *Morning News.* "I was afraid of rude signs," Connally recalled. "Or that the crowds might be hostile. I had objected to the parade route being announced well in advance because that lends itself to organized heckling. But as we neared downtown and the crowds thickened, all my fears fell away."

Announcement of the parade route by the President's advance men had brought out the crowds but it had also allowed an assassin to position himself perfectly, six stories above the route, at a sharp corner where the cars had to slow down. He was Lee Harvey Oswald, a troublemaker and political malcontent on the FBI suspect list, and a sharpshooter of deadly accuracy. In this picture, taken by his Russian wife earlier in the year, Oswald held a Trotskyite newspaper in his right hand and in his left the 6.5-mm carbine that he had bought by mail in March and would use as the murder weapon.

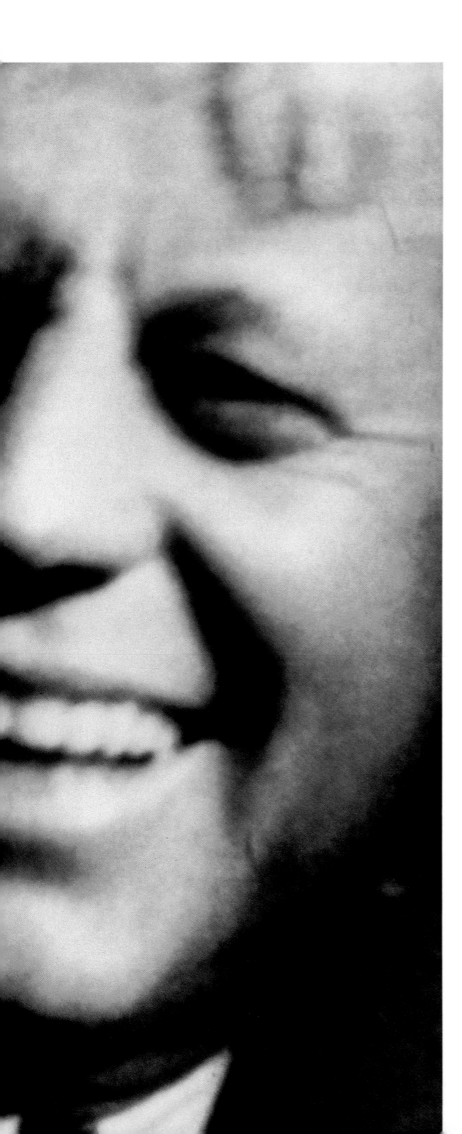

Nearing downtown Dallas

At noon the 20-car motorcade left Love Field for the seven-mile drive to downtown Dallas. On the outskirts of the city 13-year-old Chris Darrouzet took these pictures with his parents' movie camera. On shelf paper with a magic marker his aunt had scrawled PLEASE STOP AND SHAKE OUR HANDS. The limousine had almost passed Chris when it did abruptly stop and the boy recorded a last glimpse of a radiant President.

In the heart of Dallas 25 minutes away, the lunch break had just begun in the six-story book warehouse, a way station for textbooks headed for Texas schools. That morning one of the workers had arrived with a long, thin object wrapped in brown paper—"window shades," Lee Harvey Oswald had claimed.

For most of his 24 years Oswald had been out of step with the world. Born in New Orleans two months after his father had died, Oswald was boarded out at three, then yanked by his mother from city to city and school to school, his reputation as a loser and troublemaker growing with each move. An ex-Marine with two court-martials on his record, Oswald turned to Marxism and defected to Russia, only to be denied citizenship there.

After several years of disenchantment, he returned to the U.S. with a Russian bride and a baby girl. Floating from job to job, suspicious, vengeful and defiant, he purchased a mail-order rifle and had already come close to killing a public figure with it. Only five weeks before the President's visit to Texas, Oswald had been hired by the Book Depository to fill orders at $1.25 an hour.

On Nov. 22, as the Kennedy motorcade approached, Oswald finally decided to do something violent and catastrophic about all the rage he felt. As other workers ate at the cafeteria downstairs or took places either at windows or outside along the parade route, Oswald crouched behind book cartons in a sixth-floor corner. He unwrapped the brown paper from his rifle with its new telescopic sight and waited.

These three pictures were taken during the final minute before the shots

1. Seen from the fourth floor of the Book Depository, the car had just turned off from Main onto Houston Street.

2. A few seconds later the car slowly passed the Cal-Tex building, turning left onto Elm.

Sitting in the limousine on a jump seat directly in front of the President, Governor Connally had tried to carry on a conversation with Kennedy whenever there was a momentary lull. Sporadically they discussed a KENNEDY GO HOME sign along the way and what a *Houston Chronicle* political poll scheduled for the next day might show. Several years later Connally recalled these final minutes for LIFE. "There was a bright glitter to the sunshine and after a while Mrs. Kennedy slipped on a pair of sunglasses. When the President looked around, he said in a low voice, 'Take off your glasses, Jackie.' She had no way of knowing, but glasses are nearly as effective as a mask for hiding one's face and make participation in a parade almost useless. In a moment, forgetting perhaps, she slipped them back on and I heard him say in the same tone, 'Take off the glasses, Jackie.' He was watching the crowds, waving at them steadily with a stiff forearm, his right hand moving only a few inches, out from his face and back. It was a small movement and curiously formal but, I thought, quite effective. I heard a low monotone rumble from the back and then I realized he was responding—'Thank you, thank you, thank you'—over and over to people who couldn't hear him but who could sense he was answering them, who knew that contact had been made. And then he turned his head slightly and said, 'Jackie, take off your glasses.' "

The uncircled numbers in this drawing of the motorcade route show where Kennedy's car was when each of these three pictures was taken. The corresponding circled numbers indicate where the amateur photographers who took these pictures were positioned. ① was a woman mail supervisor in the Book Depository, shooting a movie camera from a window that can be seen in picture 3, two floors from the top of the warehouse and six windows from the right. ② and ③ were male spectators along the route. On the drawing ⊗ marks the spot where the assassin hid.

3. Hidden by boxes, the assassin was in the right top window of the Book Depository, now directly above Kennedy's car.

The assassin was aiming his rifle as the two large pictures below were made

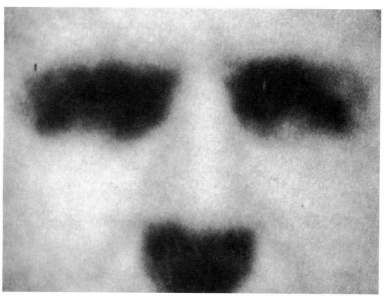

When Oswald's right eye (left) was fixed to his telescopic sight, the target he had in his cross hairs was just emerging from tree branches. For this FBI re-creation of the shooting (far left), the car with stand-ins was placed in exact position and a camera was mounted on the actual murder weapon in the sixth-floor window of the book warehouse.

The motorcade was pulling away from the Book Depository, and heading down Elm into Dealey Plaza when a spectator made the picture above. The back of Kennedy's head can be seen directly under the STEMMONS FREEWAY/KEEP RIGHT sign. To the right of the sign and directly above the head of the first Secret Service man on the running board of the security car, a couple can be seen standing on an abutment. This was Abraham Zapruder, a Dallas clothing manufacturer, and his firm's 20-year-old receptionist whom he had asked to steady him.

This picture (second left), taken only a few hours after the shooting, shows the general view Oswald had out the sixth-floor window. As the motorcade passed below the sniper's nest, Oswald braced his barrel on a carton of books and took deadly aim. The drawing at left shows the position of the President's car when the two pictures below were taken. The cameras were across the street from each other. The photographer for the picture at the left was standing at position ④. Position ⑤ marks the four-foot-high balustrade upon which Abraham Zapruder and his receptionist stood.

At almost exactly the same moment, but from the opposite side of the boulevard, the scene was recorded by Abraham Zapruder with his new Bell & Howell 8 mm movie camera. The back of the STEMMONS FREEWAY sign appears in the bottom right of the picture as the President's car begins to disappear behind it. During the full second that Kennedy was obscured by the sign, he was hit by Oswald's first bullet. On the following pages are some of the most dramatic of Zapruder's 478 frames, the most scrutinized amateur footage ever exposed.

The tiny strip of color film passed through Abraham Zapruder's 8mm movie camera at 18.3 frames per second. When Kennedy came back into view from behind the freeway sign, he had already been hit. Striking no bone, the first bullet pierced the back of his head and exited from his throat below the Adam's apple. Almost instantly his arms flew up as he grasped at the wound in his neck. Then, continuing on its flight, the bullet tunneled into Connally's back, close to the armpit. It shattered a rib, ripped open a lung, exited through his chest, smashed the Governor's right wristbone and ended up in his left leg, a few inches above the knee. Mrs. Connally remembered hearing not the slightest sound from Kennedy, but she thought she heard her husband cry out, "My God, they are going to kill us all!"

Four seconds later Mrs. Kennedy was cradling her slumping husband in her arms when the fatal bullet struck, almost hitting her as well. The bullet smashed into the right rear of Kennedy's skull, causing him to lurch backwards. "Oh, no! Oh, no!" Jackie shouted.

The first symbols of the nation's loss

The cavalcade had been laden with roses for everyone in it, but now as doctors fought vainly over the President and life slipped away, so the roses, like those here abandoned in Vice President Johnson's car, were left to wilt. At 1 o'clock on that glistening Dallas afternoon the President was pronounced dead. Within minutes, the country began to show its shock and sorrow as the Capitol flag was lowered to half-staff.

Jacqueline Kennedy followed the President's casket as it was carried into the rear of Air Force One, which waited at Love Field for the flight back to Washington.

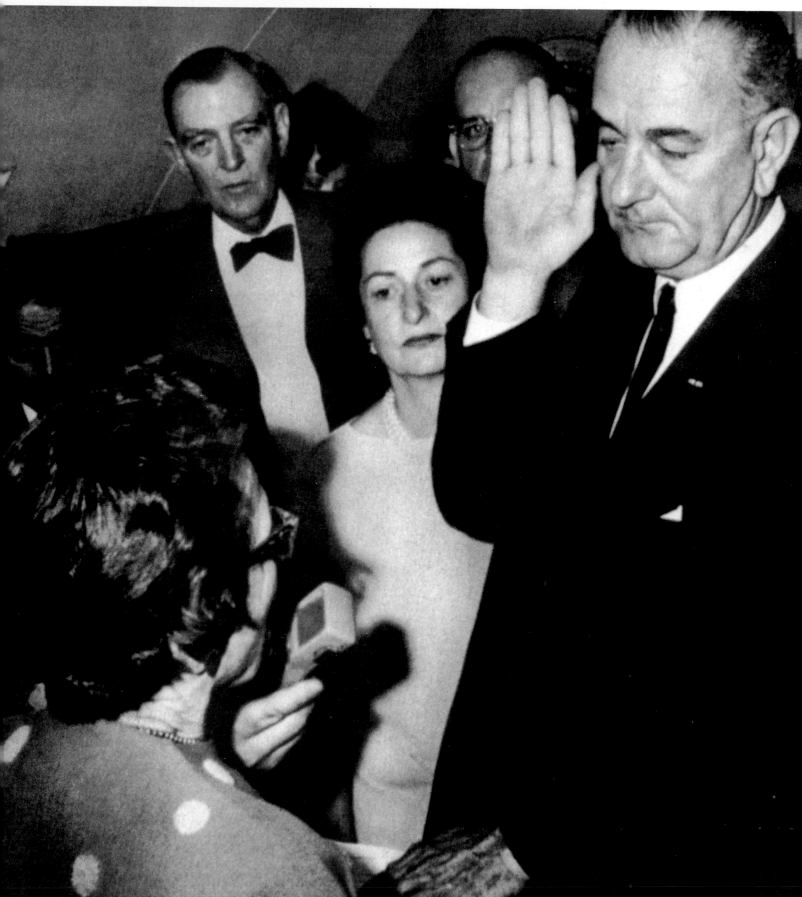

Jackie left her husband's coffin only once, to witness the swearing in of his successor

The forlorn widow joined Lady Bird and Lyndon Baines Johnson in the plane's crowded main compartment as Judge Sarah Hughes swore in the 36th President of the United States.

After the shooting an eyewitness told the police that he had seen a man poke a rifle out of a top corner window of the Book Depository and fire it at the President. His description led to Oswald's capture, and the assassin was hustled off to Dallas police headquarters just an hour before Johnson took the oath.

Clutching the hand of Bobby Kennedy, who met the plane, Jackie stayed close to her husband's casket as it was lowered on the cargo lift, then rode with it by ambulance to Bethesda Naval Hospital.

One wished for a cry, a sob . . . any human sound

by Theodore H. White LIFE, Nov. 29, 1963

No bugler sounded taps, no drum beat its ruffle, no band pealed *Hail to the Chief* as John F. Kennedy, ·35th President of the United States, returned for the last time to Washington, the city where he practiced the magic art of leadership.

It was 17 years ago he came from Boston; and, in the years since, his arrivals and departures came to punctuate the telling of American history. When he arrived, the door would open and the lithe figure would come out to give that graceful wave of the arm which became the most familiar flourish in American politics. There would follow the burst of applause, the shouts and yells, the oohs and ahs as he tripped down the stairs with that light, graceful step which was his style.

But he came this time in silence.

The faint shrill of distant jets, the sputter and cough of belly-lighted helicopters carrying the men of power from Washington to the field, the subdued conversation, all made the silence larger. It was moist and chilly and the twilight bars of pink had just given way to a quarter moon hung with mists when Air Force One,

Inside Bethesda Naval Hospital a guard of honor waited while the body was prepared for burial.

It was after 4 a.m. on Nov. 23 when a Marine honor guard marched to position in front of the White House (below). A few minutes later the ambulance bearing the President's body arrived. Jackie and Bobby were still in attendance.

the presidential jet, silently rolled up the runway from the south. The pilot in his cockpit must have sensed the hush—so skillfully had he stilled his motors, so surprisingly did the plane appear in the total glare of the lights and soundlessly come to a stop. It was 6:03 p.m.

One wished for a cry, a sob, a wail, any human sound. But the plane, white with blue flashings,

(continued)

rested under the punishment of the light—sealed and silent. A great cargo lift—glistening yellow on the outside, dazzling white on the inside, framed with lights of red and white—rolled as far as the plane; a man appeared and, for a moment, it was as it always had been: Larry O'Brien's round face peered out first. But O'Brien stooped down and, as he moved, lifted something. For the first time the ugly glint of the dark, red-bronze box showed. Behind O'Brien was Dave Powers; and then Kenny O'Donnell. These men had followed him from Boston to Washington and across the land, carrying his papers, his coats, his briefcase. This time, in last service, they carried the President himself.

They set the coffin down gently on the floor of the room-sized lift. It jounced, then steadied, then began to settle down to the

ground quietly with its burden and those from the plane who accompanied it. An honor guard of six reached out their hands to receive the coffin. The bearers bent to hand it down to them; it shook in the passing over and O'Brien's hand, almost caressing, reached out as if to steady a fragile thing or a tumbling child; then, not being needed anymore, the hand fluttered uselessly in the air.

There was, still, no voice audible except those of the broadcasters pattering as quietly as possible into their microphones. The silhouettes at the edge of the lift, cut sharp by the light, parted; and a slender woman in a rose-colored suit with dark facing appeared, then hovered at the lip of the low platform. Bobby Kennedy was there, lifting up his arms to help her down, then guiding her into the gray service ambulance with the red dome light—steady, not winking. Mrs. Kennedy's hand tried to open the ambulance door and fell limply as Bobby leaned forward, opened the door, guided her in. Then, silently, the ambulance rolled on to the north and was gone . . .

John F. Kennedy loved the noble art of politics, which is the government of men; and he would have understood that now, while his body still lay in the Bethesda Naval Hospital, where his wife and brother sat vigil, the men of Washington could not help but talk of the government of the country, of those who would carry on—which ones would the new President use, which dismiss. For there are two parts to government: the machinery, and the individuals who sit at the levers of machinery.

The machinery in Washington functioned with marvelous efficiency. By noon Saturday, less than 24 hours from the assassination of John F. Kennedy, the White House had begun to change. On Thursday, the White House staff had seized Kennedy's absence to do over again the curtains, rugs and decorations of his office; by early Friday they had finished and, even as news of his assassination came, the staff was moving furniture back where it belonged.

Saturday morning, starting at 9 a.m., all the furniture of John F. Kennedy was moved out—the desk, the paintings, the decorations, his rocking chair—leaving it as bare as when he entered, except for the two white opposing sofas by the fireplace . . .

At 4:30 in the morning, as the 1,300-pound coffin made from 500-year-old African mahogany was carried into the White House by a special detail, Jackie, still wearing her blood-spattered suit from Texas, followed closely behind.

In New York at the moment she heard the news,
a woman recoiled with the dismay and
disbelief that was universal.

Highlights of Kennedy's Care

here he was when he first heard

This was the scene on the Friday evening commuter train to Stamford, Connecticut.

Chapter 15

SAYING GOODBYE

"I am certain that, after the dust of centuries has passed over our cities, we will be remembered not for victories or defeats in battle or in politics but for our contributions to the human spirit."

by Dora Jane Hamblin LIFE Dec. 6, 1963

Throughout her long ordeal Jacqueline Kennedy's only recorded cry of pain was the "Oh, no!" she uttered as her husband was hit. From that moment on she seemed to draw strength from the events that engulfed her, until finally she imparted strength to others. Even as she waited in the hospital in Dallas, a resolve began to grow in her to erase the shame of assassination with ceremonies so dignified that the office of President would rise above its momentary emptiness. An instinct to establish the continuity of power drove her and supported her. Still in shock from the bullets that killed her husband and missed her only by inches, she stood beside the new President as he took the oath of office on the plane.

On the two hour and 21 minute flight back to Washington she had time to think. First she asked that a message be sent to Bethesda Naval Hospital asking that it be ready to prepare John Kennedy's body for burial. Then, as she sat in the rear compartment of the plane where the casket was carried, the parallel to Lincoln's death came to her mind, as it had come to so many others. Through her avid study of the White House and its residents, she knew more about it than most. From Bethesda Hospital during that first long night she began a series of astonishing detailed plans and decisions, many drawn from history, the rest of them of her own devising. LIFE's Washington Bureau Chief Henry Suydam later gathered instances of her planning.

Mrs. Kennedy asked someone to telephone a friend and send him to an upstairs library in the White House to get a specific book on Lincoln that contained photographs and drawings of ceremonies surrounding the lying-in-state and the funeral. She remembered exactly where the book was, and she told him. She wanted everything now to correspond as nearly as possible to what had been done for Lincoln. She even specified that the catafalque upon which the coffin would lie in the East Room should duplicate Lincoln's.

She did not leave the hospital until her husband's body was returned to the White House to lie in state in the East Room. She went directly there, and as dawn brightened its windows on Saturday morning she supervised the hushed-voice preparations for the catafalque and the mourning drapes. A military honor guard took up its position, and she remembered her husband's keen interest in the Special Forces, the guerrilla-trained troops he had sent to the jungles of Vietnam. She asked, "Couldn't the honor guard include a member of the Special Forces?" Soon a Special Forces man was added, wearing the green beret she had thought would be more appropriate than formal Army headgear.

It was full morning before she left her dead husband's side, and then for the most painful duty of all: to see her children for the first time and to try to find the words to tell them what had happened. In mid-morning Mrs. Kennedy returned to the East Room, this time to attend a special family mass in front of the casket. Only then did she consent to rest for a while.

During the funeral march, by a tradition that is as old as Genghis Khan, the dead President was followed by a riderless horse carrying empty boots reversed in the stirrups, in token that the warrior would not mount again.

The watching nation did not see Jacqueline Kennedy again until Sunday morning, when she and her children prepared to follow the flag-draped casket in a cortege to the rotunda of the Capitol. By then the television audience was watching Dallas' second assassination. From this primitive violence the watchers could turn to see Mrs. Kennedy, in a black suit and black lace mantilla, walking out

(continued)

At Jackie's instruction, funeral mass cards were printed on White House stationery. In her own handwriting she wrote "Dear God, please take care of your servant John Fitzgerald Kennedy" and then indicated that excerpts from the President's Inaugural Address be printed as well.

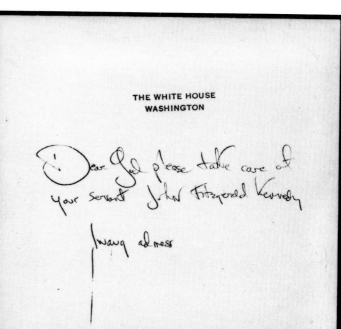

THE WHITE HOUSE
WASHINGTON

Dear God please take care of your servant John Fitzgerald Kennedy

Inaug address

of the White House and up the 36 marble steps of the Capitol. There was no hand at her shoulder, no veil to hide her face. With each gloved hand she held a small hand, and her quiet eyes were fixed on the casket moving slowly up the steps ahead of her. She and the children moved into place in the vast rotunda. Caroline was solemn and still. John-

John, as his father had nicknamed him, gazed with interest at the soldiers and craned at the dome, then began to visit with the dignitaries so amiably and audibly that he was hustled off to the office of the Speaker of the House.

Once or twice, as the sonorous eulogies echoed in the chamber, Mrs. Kennedy swayed

slightly. From time to time she touched her face, but it seemed no more than the familiar gesture she had always used to brush her hair lightly away. Caroline once let go of her mother's hand and began tapping her gloved fingertips together. Her mother reached down gently and took her hand again. Then, in a silent moment of dignity and courage

From 4:30 Saturday morning until Sunday afternoon, President Kennedy lay in state in the East Room of the White House. Then the casket was moved to the Capitol rotunda. There—around the same catafalque on which Abraham Lincoln had lain— the solemnities began. Present were U.S. Senators and Representatives, members of the Cabinet and the Supreme Court, U.S. delegates to the U.N., the White House staff and foreign dignitaries. Withheld by the networks until the ceremonies were over was the stunning news of the death of Oswald (below), gunned down by Dallas nightclub operator Jack Ruby as the assassin was being moved from jail.

that helped to redeem the second moment of madness in Dallas, the two walked to the bier and knelt beside it.

As they left the rotunda, John-John joined them again, clutching two small flags in his right hand. He had been given one, in the Speaker's office, to entertain him, and he asked for the other one "for my Daddy."

All during that ceremony at the Capitol, Jacqueline Kennedy's first appearance since she had walked into the White House in her bloodstained clothing 32 hours before, she relied both on her sense of history and upon details "that the President would have liked." He had loved his Navy years, and she asked that the Navy hymn be played at

the Capitol while his casket was being carried up the stairs.

A sense of history and a sure knowledge of her husband's wishes would guide her plans for the next day as well. She remembered his delight at the concert they had all heard on the White House lawn on Veterans Day, when the Black Watch bagpipers played, and she asked that

(continued)

they form a part of his funeral cortege. She remembered her husband telling her about an Irish Guard funeral drill he had seen last June in Dublin as he laid a wreath on a monument to the Irish Rebellion. She asked for such a drill at his funeral.

As the movers came to clear the presidential Oval Office of her husband's effects, she even remembered that he had promised, a month ago, to give his

desk telephone to the Army Signal Corps at Fort Monmouth, New Jersey, because he had used it last August to initiate the Army's Syncom satellite. She asked that someone please see to it that the telephone was delivered to the fort.

Much of this planning had been done by Saturday evening when thousands of people were already lining up at the Capitol, waiting to pay last respects to

John Kennedy. Suddenly, Sunday evening, as the mourners were shuffling through the rotunda, Jacqueline wanted to go back there herself. She asked Robert Kennedy, who had barely left her side, to take her back. They walked in unannounced, at about 9 p.m., and went so quietly to the coffin that hardly anyone noticed them. While Robert waited behind the rope that isolated the catafalque from the

crowds, Mrs. Kennedy knelt again beside it for a few moments, again touching the flag with her lips.

Then she rose, stepped back and looked at the faces in the silent, shuffling crowd. Her brother-in-law touched her arm and they walked out together. The night air had grown very cold. Robert urged her toward a waiting limousine but she said, "Let me walk, let me walk."

They stepped into the darkness together. A woman who recognized her stepped forward impulsively and hugged her. Mrs. Kennedy reached up her arms and hugged her in return, without words. She stopped for a moment to speak to some nuns and walked on, coatless in the cold. Then the crowds all saw her at once, and Robert and the Secret Service men guided her back to the car.

Outside, a quarter of a million people were lining up to file past the coffin, all night long in a silent stream.

After brief eulogies Mrs. Kennedy and her daughter Caroline knelt at the President's coffin. Instinctively, the little girl's hand tenderly fumbled under the flag to reach closer.

It was the final journey now and the whole of America watched and heard and trembled

For Jackie, Caroline and John Jr., Monday's solemn pageantry began at this moment on the steps of the White House.

The caisson was drawn by three pairs of matched gray horses from the Capitol to the White House and then, with the Kennedy family behind, to St. Matthew's Cathedral. Following military custom, the right row of horses was saddled but riderless.

The caisson stood empty beside St. Matthew's as the funeral mass was said inside. Jackie broke down once during the service, but by the time she reappeared with her children at the Cathedral doors (right) she had regained her composure.

At the funeral, there was Luigi Vena of Boston, singing *Ave Maria* just as he had sung it 10 years before when John Kennedy wed Jacqueline Bouvier.

The funeral mass and then across the Potomac to a hill in Arlington

Leaving Washington and the Lincoln Memorial behind, the three-mile-long procession made its way across the Potomac toward Arlington Cemetery.

Creaking wheels and clattering hoofs broke the silence as the caisson entered the cemetery and passed the graves of American war heroes.

AN EPILOGUE

LIFE, Dec. 9, 1963
Hyannis Port

The eternal flame at the floodlit grave glowed amid banks of flowers. Above it stands the Custis-Lee mansion where General Robert E. Lee once lived.

She remembers how hot the sun was in Dallas, and the crowds—greater and wilder than the crowds in Mexico or in Vienna. The sun was blinding, streaming down; yet she could not put on sunglasses for she had to wave to the crowd.

And up ahead she remembers seeing a tunnel around a turn and thinking that there would be a moment of coolness under the tunnel. There was the sound of motorcycles, as always in a parade, and the occasional backfire of a motorcycle. The sound of the shot came, at that moment, like the sound of a backfire and she remembers Connally saying, "No, no, no, no, no. . ."

She remembers the roses. Three times that day in Texas they had been greeted with the bouquets of yellow roses of Texas. Only, in Dallas they had given her *red* roses. She remembers thinking, how funny—red roses for me; and then the car was full of blood and red roses.

Much later, accompanying the body from the Dallas hospital to the airport, she was alone with Clint Hill—the first Secret Service man to come to their rescue—and with Dr. Burkley, the White House physician. Burkley gave her two roses that had slipped under the President's shirt when he fell, his head in her lap.

All through the night they tried to separate him from her, to sedate her, and take care of her—and she would not let them. She wanted to be with him. She remembered that Jack had said of his father, when his father suffered the stroke, that he could not live like that. Don't let that happen to me, he had said, when I have to go.

Now, in her hand she was holding a gold St. Christopher's medal.

She had given him a St. Christopher's medal when they were married; but when Patrick died this summer, they had wanted to put something in the coffin with Patrick that was from them both; so he had put in the St. Christopher's medal.

Then he had asked her to give him a new one to

By Theodore H. White

mark their 10th wedding anniversary, a month after Patrick's death.

He was carrying it when he died and she had found it. But it belonged to him—so she could not put *that* in the coffin with him. She wanted to give him something that was hers, something that she loved. So she had slipped off her wedding ring and put it on his finger. When she came out of the room in the hospital in Dallas, she asked: "Do you think it was right? Now I have nothing left." And Kenny O'Donnell said, "You leave it where it is."

That was at 1:30 p.m. in Texas.

But then, at Bethesda Hospital in Maryland, at 3 a.m. the next morning, Kenny slipped into the chamber where the body lay and brought her back the ring, which, as she talked now, she twisted.

On her little finger was the other ring: a slim, gold circlet with green emerald chips—the one he had given her in memory of Patrick.

There was a thought, too, that was always with her. "When Jack quoted something, it was usually classical," she said, "but I'm so ashamed of myself—all I could keep thinking of is this line from a musical comedy.

"At night, before we'd go to sleep, Jack liked to play some records; and the song he loved most came at the very end of this record. The lines he loved to hear were: *Don't let it be forgot, that once there was a spot, for one brief shining moment that was known as Camelot.*"

She wanted to make sure that the point came clear and went on: "There'll be great Presidents again—and the Johnsons are wonderful, they've been wonderful to me—but there'll never be another Camelot again.

"Once, the more I read of history the more bitter I got. For a while I thought history was something that bitter old men wrote. But then I realized history made Jack what he was. You must think of him as this little boy, sick so much of the time, reading in bed, reading history, reading the Knights of the Round Table, reading Marlborough. For Jack, history was full of heroes. And if it made him this way—if it made him see the heroes—maybe other little boys will see. Men are such a combination of good and bad. Jack had this hero idea of history, the idealistic view."

But she came back to the idea that transfixed her: "*Don't let it be forgot, that once there was a spot, for one brief shining moment that was known as Camelot*—and it will never be that way again."

As for herself? She was horrified by the stories that she might live abroad. "I'm *never* going to live in Europe. I'm not going to 'travel extensively abroad.' That's a desecration. I'm going to live in the places I lived with Jack. In Georgetown, and with the Kennedys at the Cape. They're my family. I'm going to bring up my children. I want John to grow up to be a good boy."

As for the President's memorial, at first she remembered that, in every speech in their last days in Texas, he had spoken of how in December this nation would loft the largest rocket booster yet into the sky, making us first in space. So she had wanted something of his there when it went up—perhaps only his initials painted on a tiny corner of the great Saturn, where no one need even notice it. But now Americans will seek the moon from Cape Kennedy. The new name, born of her frail hope, came as a surprise.

The only thing she knew she must have for him was the eternal flame over his grave at Arlington.

"Whenever you drive across the bridge from Washington into Virginia," she said, "you see the Lee Mansion on the side of the hill in the distance. When Caroline was very little, the mansion was one of the first things she learned to recognize. Now, at night you can see his flame beneath the mansion for miles away."

She said it is time people paid attention to the new President and the new First Lady. But she does not want them to forget John F. Kennedy or read of him only in dusty or bitter histories:

For one brief shining moment there was Camelot.

This was the President's favorite photograph. He loved to walk on the dunes near Hyannis Port. And this was his son's farewell salute—facing his father's coffin and doing what he had seen the real soldiers do.

This is how LIFE ended its special J.F.K. memorial edition following the assassination. In this retelling of Camelot so many years later, it still seems fitting to let these two pictures close the story. This is how it was, you can tell your children, and your children's children. And tell them too, that, ever since, nothing has quite been the same.

LIFE's funeral issue marked the 21st time the Kennedy story appeared on the magazine's cover. Since then there have been 27 more Kennedy covers. Seen together they create a vivid compendium of the ongoing triumphs and tragedies of this remarkable American family.

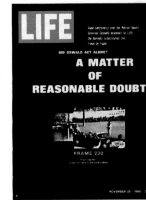

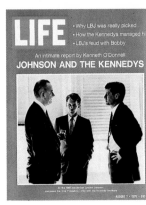

CREDITS

Photographers' credits are listed page by page and separated left to right by semi-colons, from top to bottom by dashes. Images appearing within reproduced pages of the magazine are not listed
—————————
All photographs and art work are protected by copyright, except those credited to agencies of the U.S. government. Time Inc. owns the copyright to all images credited to "LIFE".

4: Ed Clark, LIFE. **5:** Bachrach, Inc. **6:** No Credit. **7:** Wide World. **8:** No Credit. **9:** No Credit—Paul Schutzer, LIFE—Art Rickerby, LIFE. **10:** No Credit—Allan Grant, LIFE. **16:** Black Star. **17:** Brown Brothers—No Credit—Boston Record American. **18:** Brown Brothers. **19:** Wide World. **20:** Bettmann Archive/Underwood & Underwood. **21:** No Credit. **22:** Pictures, Inc.—Wide World; Wide World—Wide World. **23:** No Credit—Wide World; Pictures, Inc.—Wide World. **24:** No Credit. **26:** Wide World—Bettmann/UPI. **27:** No Credit. **28:** Wide World. **29:** No Credit. **30:** No Credit. **31:** Al Fenn, LIFE. **33:** Yale Joel, LIFE. **34:** Yale Joel, LIFE. **36:** Yale Joel, LIFE; Allan Grant, LIFE—Yale Joel, LIFE—Yale Joel, LIFE. **37:** Yale Joel, LIFE. **38:** Hy Peskin. **39:** Hy Peskin. **40:** Hy Peskin. **41:** Hy Peskin (all). **42:** Hy Peskin. **44:** Hy Peskin. **45:** Hy Peskin. **46:** Hy Peskin (all). **47:** Hy Peskin. **48:** Lisa Larsen. **50:** Lisa Larsen (all). **51:** Lisa Larsen (all). **52:** Lisa Larsen (all). **53:** Lisa Larsen (all). **54:** Lisa Larsen (all). **55:** Lisa Larsen; Lisa Larsen—Toni Frissel; Lisa Larsen; Lisa Larsen—Lisa Larsen; Lisa Larsen. **56:** Lisa Larsen; Lisa Larsen—Lisa Larsen; Toni Frissel—Lisa Larsen; Lisa Larsen. **57:** Lisa Larsen (all). **58:** Lisa Larsen (all). **59:** Lisa Larsen. **60:** Lisa Larsen. **61:** Lisa Larsen (all). **62:** Howard Sochurek, LIFE—Howard Sochurek, LIFE. **63:** Howard Sochurek, LIFE. **64:** Howard Sochurek, LIFE (all). **65:** Howard Sochurek, LIFE. **66:** Alfred Eisenstaedt, LIFE; Alfred Eisenstaedt, LIFE—Hank Walker, LIFE; Hank Walker, LIFE. **67:** Howard Sochurek, LIFE. **68:** Howard Sochurek, LIFE (all). **69:** Howard Sochurek, LIFE (all). **70:** Francis Miller, LIFE. **71:** Alfred Eisenstaedt, LIFE. **73:** Carl Mydans, LIFE. **74:** Bradford Bachrach. **75:** Howard Sochurek, LIFE. **76:** (c) Mark Shaw Collection/Photo Researchers. **78:** Nina Leen. **79:** Nina Leen. **80:** Ed Clark, LIFE. **81:** Ed Clark, LIFE. **82:** Ed Clark, LIFE. **84:** (c) Mark Shaw Collection/Photo Research-

ers (all). **85:** (c) Mark Shaw Collection/Photo Researchers. **86:** (c) Mark Shaw Collection/Photo Researchers. **88:** (c) Mark Shaw Collection/Photo Researchers. **89:** (c) Mark Shaw Collection/Photo Researchers (all). **90:** (c) Mark Shaw Collection/Photo Researchers. **92:** (c) Mark Shaw Collection/Photo Researchers. **93:** (c) Mark Shaw Collection/Photo Researchers (all). **94:** Hank Walker, LIFE. **95:** Robert Kelley, LIFE. **96:** Robert Kelley, LIFE (all). **97:** Stan Wayman, LIFE. **98:** Stan Wayman, LIFE. **99:** Stan Wayman, LIFE. **100:** Stan Wayman, LIFE. **102:** Stan Wayman, LIFE (all). **103:** Stan Wayman, LIFE (all). **104:** Hank Walker, LIFE. **105:** Hank Walker, LIFE. **106:** Hank Walker, LIFE (all). **107:** Hank Walker, LIFE (all). **108:** Hank Walker, LIFE. **109:** Hank Walker, LIFE. **110:** Hank Walker, LIFE. **111:** Hank Walker, LIFE. **112:** Ed Clark, LIFE (all). **113:** Ed Clark, LIFE. **114:** Ralph Crane, LIFE. **116:** Hank Walker, LIFE—Ralph Crane, LIFE. **117:** Hank Walker, LIFE (all). **118:** Hank Walker, LIFE. **119:** Francis Miller, LIFE (all). **120:** Hank Walker, LIFE (all). **121:** Hank Walker, LIFE. **122:** Hank Walker, LIFE (all). **123:** Hank Walker, LIFE; Howard Sochurek, LIFE—Hank Walker, LIFE. **124:** Howard Sochurek, LIFE; Wide World—Ted Polumbaum. **125:** Francis Miller, LIFE. **126:** Paul Schutzer,

LIFE. **127:** Paul Schutzer, LIFE. **128:** Paul Schutzer, LIFE (all). **129:** Paul Schutzer, LIFE. **130:** Paul Schutzer, LIFE. **132:** Paul Schutzer, LIFE. **134:** Paul Schutzer, LIFE (all). **135:** Paul Schutzer, LIFE. **136:** Paul Schutzer, LIFE. **138:** Paul Schutzer, LIFE. **140:** Paul Schutzer, LIFE (all). Paul Schutzer, LIFE. **141:** Paul Schutzer, LIFE. **142:** Paul Schutzer, LIFE. **143:** Paul Schutzer, LIFE. **144:** Paul Schutzer, LIFE. **146:** Paul Schutzer, LIFE (all). **147:** Paul Schutzer, LIFE. **148:** Paul Schutzer, LIFE (all). **150:** Paul Schutzer, LIFE. **152:** Paul Schutzer, LIFE. **154:** Paul Schutzer, LIFE. **156:** Paul Schutzer, LIFE. **157:** Hank Walker, LIFE. **158:** Art Rickerby, LIFE. **159:** Paul Schutzer, LIFE. **160:** Phil Stern. **162:** George Silk, LIFE. **163:** Leonard McCombe, LIFE—Alfred Eisenstaedt, LIFE; Frank Scherschel, LIFE. **166:** Ed Clark, LIFE (all). **167:** Ed Clark, LIFE (all). **168:** Alfred Eisenstaedt, LIFE. **169:** Paul Schutzer, LIFE. **170:** George Silk, LIFE. **171:** Joe Scherschel, LIFE. **172:** Joe Scherschel, LIFE. **174:** Paul Schutzer, LIFE. **175:** George Silk, LIFE. **176:** Paul Schutzer, LIFE. **177:** Joe Scherschel, LIFE. **178:** George Silk, LIFE. **180:** Paul Schutzer, LIFE. **181:** Joe Scherschel, LIFE. **182:** Paul Schutzer, LIFE. **184:** Paul Schutzer, LIFE. **186:** Leonard McCombe, LIFE; Art Rickerby, LIFE—Art Rickerby, LIFE—Art Rick-

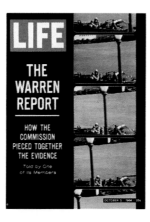

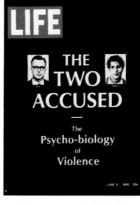

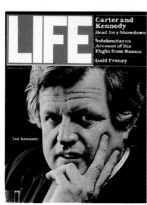

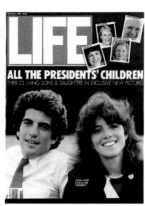

erby, LIFE—Art Rickerby, LIFE. **187:** Al Fenn, LIFE. **190:** Leonard McCombe, LIFE (all). **191:** Frank Scherschel, LIFE—Alfred Eisenstaedt, LIFE. **192:** Leonard McCombe, LIFE. **193:** Leonard McCombe, LIFE. **194:** Ed Clark, LIFE. **195:** Paul Schutzer, LIFE. **196:** (c) Mark Shaw Collection/Photo Researchers. **198:** Alfred Eisenstaedt, LIFE—Carl Iwasaki; Ed Clark, LIFE. **199:** Don Uhrbrock; Tommy Weber. **200:** Ed Clark, LIFE—Frank Scherschel, LIFE—Alfred Eisenstaedt, LIFE. **201:** Alfred Eisenstaedt, LIFE (all top row)—Grey Villet, LIFE; Paul Schutzer, LIFE. **202:** George Silk, LIFE. **203:** George Silk, LIFE—Drawing by Adolph E. Brotman. **204:** Nina Leen; Ed Clark, LIFE—Ed Clark, LIFE—Nina Leen. **205:** Ed Clark, LIFE. **206:** Joe Scherschel, LIFE—Fred Ward, Black Star. **207:** Michael Rougier, LIFE. **208:** Paul Schutzer, LIFE (all). **209:** Neil Leifer, Time Inc. **210:** Robert Halmi. **211:** Warner Bros. **210:** Al Fenn, LIFE—Yale Joel, LIFE (all). **212:** Bert and Richard Morgan Studio—Marshall Hawkins—Marshall Hawkins. **213:** Marshall Hawkins. **214:** Cecil W. Stoughton, White House Photographer. **215:** Yale Joel—Cecil W. Stoughton, White House Photographer. **216:** Ralph Morse, LIFE—Bob Gomel. **217:** Al Fenn, LIFE—Leonard McCombe, LIFE. **218:** Art Rickerby, LIFE (all). **219:** Art Rickerby,

LIFE. **220:** Bill Beebe, Los Angeles Times. **221:** Bettmann/UPI—Bill Eppridge, LIFE. **222:** John Dominis, LIFE (all). **223:** John Dominis, LIFE (all). **224:** (c) Mark Shaw Collection/Photo Researchers (all). **225:** (c) Mark Shaw Collection/Photo Researchers. **226:** Cecil W. Stoughton, White House Photographer. **228:** Paul Schutzer, LIFE. **229:** Paul Schutzer, LIFE. **230:** Ed Clark, LIFE—Wide World. **232:** Charles Moore, Black Star—Charles Moore, Black Star—Lynn Pelham. **233:** Art Rickerby, LIFE. **234:** James Mahan. **236:** James Mahan. **237:** U.S. Dept. of Defense. **238:** U.S. Dept. of Defense. **239:** Wide World; Bettmann/UPI—U.S. Dept. of Defense. **240:** Ed Clark, LIFE; Lynn Pelham. **241:** Paul Schutzer, LIFE (all). **242:** Bob Gomel. **243:** Dan Bernstein. **244:** Paul Schutzer, LIFE. **246:** Leonard McCombe, LIFE. **247:** Paul Schutzer, LIFE (all). **248:** Pierre Boulat. **249:** Hank Walker, LIFE. **250:** Paul Schutzer, LIFE (all). **251:** Paul Schutzer, LIFE. **252:** Paul Schutzer, LIFE. **254:** Art Rickerby, LIFE; John Dominis, LIFE. **255:** John Dominis, LIFE. **256:** Art Rickerby, LIFE. **258:** Art Rickerby, LIFE. **259:** Art Rickerby, LIFE. **260:** Art Rickerby, LIFE. **262:** Peter Anderson. **263:** Bettmann/UPI. **264:** John Dominis, LIFE (all). **265:** John Dominis, LIFE (all). **266:** John Dominis, LIFE (all). **267:** John Dominis, LIFE (all).

268: John Dominis, LIFE. **270:** Art Rickerby, LIFE. **272:** Art Rickerby, LIFE (all). **273:** Art Rickerby, LIFE (all). **274:** Art Rickerby, LIFE. **275:** Art Rickerby, LIFE (all). **276:** Art Rickerby, LIFE. **277:** No Credit. **278:** Christopher Darouzet (all). **279:** No Credit. **280:** Elsie Dorman; drawing by Time Inc.—James K. Towner. **281:** Robert J. Hughes. **282:** National Archives; No Credit—Hugh Betzner. **283:** Flip Schulke, Black Star; drawing by Time Inc.—Abraham Zapruder. **284-285:** Abraham Zapruder (all). **286-287:** Abraham Zapruder (all). **288-289:** Abraham Zapruder (all). **290:** Ed Clark, LIFE. **291:** Art Rickerby, LIFE. **292:** Cecil W. Stoughton, White House Photographer (all). **293:** Jim Murray—Wide World—Wide World. **294:** Robert Phillips. **295:** Fred Ward, Black Star (all). **296:** Cecil Stoughton, White House Photographer. **298:** Stan Wayman, LIFE. **299:** Carl Mydans, LIFE. **301:** No Credit—Fred Ward, Black Star. **302:** Wide World; Bob Gomel. **304:** Bob Gomel. **305:** Art Rickerby, LIFE—Henri Dauman (c) 1963. **306:** Fred Ward, Black Star. **307:** Bob Gomel—Fred Ward, Black Star. **308:** Bob Gomel; George Silk, LIFE—Art Rickerby, LIFE. **309:** Stan Wayman, LIFE—John Loengard, LIFE. **310:** Stan Wayman, LIFE—Bob Gomel. **311:** Stan Wayman, LIFE (all). **312:** Enrico

Sarsini. **313:** Paul Schutzer, LIFE; David Lees—Marvin W. Schwartz—Terence Spencer. **314:** George Silk, LIFE. **315-316 magazine pages:** (c) Mark Shaw Collection/Photo Researchers. **318-319 LIFE Covers:** 2/21/64: No Credit; 5/29/64: George Silk, LIFE; 7/3/64: George Silk, LIFE—7/10/64: No Credit; 10/2/64: Abraham Zapruder; 1/15/65: Leonard McCombe, LIFE; 4/9/65: No Credit; 7/16/65: (c) Mark Shaw Collection, Photo Researchers; 11/5/65: Portrait by James Fosburgh; 5/6/66: Blanco Y Negro; 11/18/66: Bill Eppridge, LIFE; 11/25/66: Abraham Zapruder; 11/17/67: Larry Burrows, LIFE; 11/24/67: John Dominis, LIFE; inset by Zintgraf. 6/14/68: Bill Eppridge, LIFE.—6/21/68: Wide World (left), Bettmann/UPI (right); 11/1/68: Bill Ray, LIFE; 8/1/69: John Loengard, LIFE; 7/17/70: Leonard McCombe, LIFE; 8/7/70: (c) Jacques Lowe; 2/12/71: Ron Galella; 6/11/71: Henry Grossman; 3/31/72: Art Zelin, Globe; 11/79: Co Rentmeester; 11/83: Alfred Eisenstaedt, LIFE, insets by Art Rickerby, LIFE, Abraham Zapruder, Cecil W. Stoughton, Fred Ward/Black Star, Jack Beers/Dallas Morning News, Henri Dauman, Wide World; 11/84: Harry Benson (all); 9/86: Harry Benson, inset by Press Association.